# WILD swimming
# *Walks*

LAKE DISTRICT
28 lake, river & waterfall
days out

*Happy Swimming! :)*

*Pete Kelly*

Pete Kelly

WILD
THINGS
PUBLISHING

# **WILD** swimming
# *Walks*

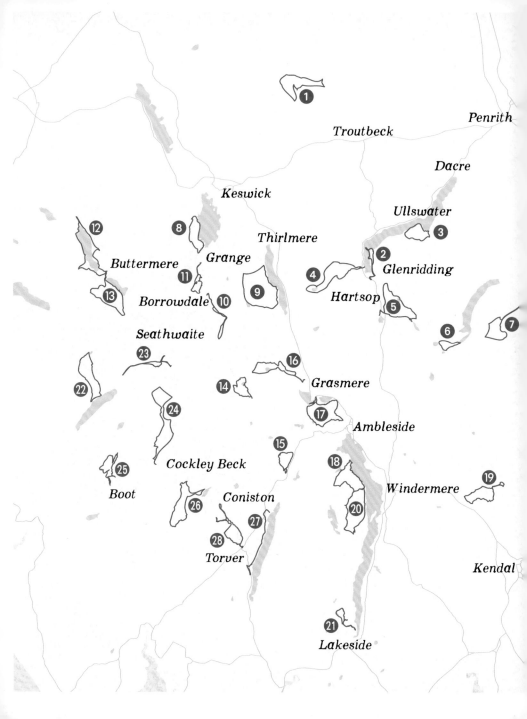

# THE WALKS

*Tebay*

# TABLE OF WALKS

| No. | NAME | SWIMMING | SWIMMING TYPE |
| --- | --- | --- | --- |
| 1 | River Caldew and Bowscale Tarn | River Caldew and Bowscale Tarn | River and Tarn |
| 2 | Silver Bay and the Ullswater Islands | Ullswater | Lake |
| 3 | Howtown, Sandwick and Kailpot Crag | Ullswater | Lake and Jumps |
| 4 | Helvellyn, Red Tarn, Glenridding Beck and Ullswater | Red Tarn, Glenridding Beck and Ullswater | Tarn, Dubs and Lake |
| 5 | The Tarns of Patterdale and Hartsop | Brothers Water, Hayeswater and Angle Tarn | Tarns |
| 6 | Blea Water and Small Water | Blea Water and Small Water | Tarns |
| 7 | The Falls of Swindale | Force Falls | Waterfalls and Dubs |
| 8 | Cat Bells and the Derwentwater Shoreline | Derwentwater | Lake |
| 9 | Harrop and Blea Tarn | Harrop and Blea Tarn | Tarns |
| 10 | Blackmoor Pot, Galleny Force and The Fairy Glen | Langstrath Beck | Waterfalls and Dubs |
| 11 | Castle Crag, the River Derwent and Millican Dalton's Cave | River Derwent | River |
| 12 | Crummock Water and Scale Force | Crummock Water and Scale Force | Lake, Waterfalls and Dubs |
| 13 | Bleaberry Tarn, High Stile and Buttermere | Bleaberry Tarn and Buttermere | Tarn and Lake |
| 14 | Stickle Tarn and the Langdale Pikes | Stickle Gill and Stickle Tarn | Tarn and Dubs |
| 15 | Yew Tree Tarn, the Holme Fell Tarns and Hodge Close Quarry | Holme Fell Tarns and Hodge Close Quarry | Tarns and Quarries |
| 16 | Sour Milk Gill, Easedale and Codale Tarns | Sour Milk Gill, Easedale and Codale Tarns | Tarns and Dubs |
| 17 | The Vale of the Lake District Poets | Loughrigg Tarn, Grasmere and Rydal Water | Lakes |
| 18 | Wray Castle, Windermere, and the Latterbarrow Ramble | Windermere | Lake |
| 19 | Staveley, the River Kent and the Tarns of Potter Fell | Potter Tarn, Gurnal Dubs and the River Kent | River and Tarns |
| 20 | Windermere, Moss Eccles and Wise Een Tarn | Windermere, Moss Eccles and Wise Een Tarn | Tarns |
| 21 | Finsthwaite, High Dam and the River Leven | High Dam and the River Leven | River and Tarn |
| 22 | Scoat Tarn and Low Tarn | Scoat Tarn and Low Tarn | Tarns |
| 23 | The Emerald Pool, Sprinkling Tarn and Styhead Tarn | The Emerald Pool, Sprinkling Tarn and Styhead Tarn | Tarns and Dubs |
| 24 | Upper Esk and Scafell Pike | Upper River Esk | River, Waterfalls and Dubs |
| 25 | Blea Tarn at Beckfoot | Blea Tarn, Whillan Beck Force, Gill Force, Stanley Force and the River Esk | Tarn, Waterfalls and Dubs |
| 26 | The Duddon Valley and Seathwaite Tarn | River Duddon and Seathwaite Tarn | River and Tarn |
| 27 | Coniston Launch Adventure | Coniston | Lake |
| 28 | Blind Tarn, Goats Water and the Tranearth Pool | Blind Tarn, Goats Water and Tranearth Pool | Tarns |

| TERRAIN | TRAVEL | START POINT | MILES | DIFFICULTY |
|---|---|---|---|---|
| Moderate roadside and fell walking | Train & bus | NY 356 322 | 7.1 | Moderate |
| Easy fell walking on good tracks and trails | Train & bus | NY 395 159 | 4.6 | Easy |
| Easy fell walking on good tracks and trails | Train & bus | NY 443 199 | 3.8 | Easy |
| Hard fell walking with some easy scrambling in high mountain terrain | Train, bus & boat | NY 385 169 | 8.4 | Hard |
| Hard fell walking in high mountain terrain | Train & bus | NY 403 133 | 6.2 | Hard |
| Moderate fell walking, steep ground in places | Car or taxi | NY 469 107 | 3.0 | Moderate |
| Moderate fell walking on reasonable tracks and trails | Car or taxi | NY 521 144 | 7.2 | Moderate |
| Moderate fell walking on good tracks and trails | Train, bus & boat | NY 246 211 | 5.0 | Moderate |
| Hard fell walking in high mountain boggy terrain, steep ground in places | Train & bus | NY 315 140 | 7.5 | Hard |
| Moderate fell walking on good tracks and trails, although a big day out | Train & bus | NY 257 148 | 6.2 | Moderate |
| Easy fell walking on wooded tracks and trails | Train & bus | NY 254 174 | 5.3 | Easy |
| Moderate, undulating fell walking on rough and often boggy ground | Train & bus | NY 149 215 | 9.0 | Moderate |
| Hard fell walking in high mountain terrain, steep ground in places | Train & bus | NY 174 169 | 7.1 | Hard |
| Moderate to hard fell walking in high mountain terrain, steep ground in places | Train & bus | NY 295 064 | 3.1 | Moderate |
| Easy to moderate fell walking in pleasant, mixed terrain | Train, bus & taxi | NY 322 003 | 3.6 | Moderate |
| Moderate fell walking to remote tarn | Train & bus | NY 336 075 | 6.2 | Moderate |
| Easy to moderate fell walking on good roads, tracks and trails. | Train & bus | NY 364 062 | 6.8 | Moderate |
| Easy fell walking in pleasant, mixed terrain | Train, bus & boat | NY 375 010 | 5.5 | Easy |
| Moderate fell walking on good roads, tracks and trails | Train & bus | SD 472 981 | 6.1 | Moderate |
| Moderate fell walking through mixed terrain on good roads, tracks and trails | Train, bus & ferry | SD 378 953 | 6.1 | Moderate |
| Easy to moderate fell walking through mixed terrain on good roads, tracks and trails | Train & taxi | SD 378 873 | 4.1 | Easy |
| Hard fell walking in high mountain terrain to remote tarns | Train & taxi | NY 168 068 | 6.2 | Hard |
| Moderate fell walking to mountin tarns | Train & taxi | NY 186084 | 7.1 | Moderate |
| Hard fell walking in high mountain terrain with steep ground, return along river valley | Train & taxi | NY 213 011 | 10.5 | Hard |
| A big day of moderate fell walking on varied terrain | Train & taxi | NY 173 007 | 6.5 | Moderate |
| Moderate fell walking to high tarn returning along river valley | Train & taxi | SD 235 995 | 7.7 | Moderate |
| Motor launch journey by lake, returning via easy lakeshore walk | Train & bus | SD 307 970 | 5.0 | Easy |
| Moderate- to hard fell walking to mountain tarns | Train & bus | SD 284 942 | 7.7 | Hard |

7

# INTRODUCTION

There is nowhere on this good green Earth quite like the English Lake District. Forged by the Ice Age, conquered by the Romans and named by the Vikings it has a unique heritage and sense of place, evident in the fierce sense of belonging to all who call this place home. Of course, the Lakes has a long association with mountaineering and fell walking, but also with outdoor swimming. Since the time of William Wordsworth (1770 – 1850) and Samuel Taylor Coleridge (1772 – 1834), visitors to the region have enjoyed taking to the waters as part of a vigorous and stimulating outdoor life.

As a swimming destination in itself, the Lake District is in a class of its own. The long, narrow ribbon lakes carved out by the glaciers, and the tarns, gills, becks and rivers that feed them, were all made for swimming, and in such surroundings! There are larger and more imposing mountains in Britain, but none have the beauty and grace of the Lake District Fells. It is plain to see how the dramatic scenery of the Lakes inspired some of our most lauded artists and poets to create their finest work. To gaze upon any painting by William Heaton Cooper (1903 - 1995), or to become immersed in William Wordsworth's epic poem The Prelude is to be transported to the very edge of the falls at Blackmoss Pot (known in Heaton Cooper's time as Blackmoor Pot), or to the craggy shoreline and eminently swimmable waters of Ullswater. These works reflect a deep understanding of the natural world, which is perhaps why we love them so much, created as they are, in Wordsworth's words, by "nurslings of the mountains" and "wanderers among the woods and fields": in other words, by people to whom we can relate.

## THE LAKE DISTRICT POETS

Lakeland has so many associations with the literary and artistic comets of our nation that it is impossible to do them justice in a mere introduction. It is hoped that by directing the reader to the very same becks, tarns, lakes and mountainsides that they once enjoyed, the joy of being literally and figuratively immersed in the surroundings can be fully appreciated. To swim in the Vale of the Lake District Poets, within a stone's throw from Dove Cottage and de Quincey's Opium Room can't fail to add a touch of romance to a day out in the Lakes.

The Lake Poets all lived in the Lakes and were considered to be part of the Romantic Movement, which they went on to define in their own individual way. The core of the group comprised William Wordsworth, Samuel Taylor Coleridge, and Robert Southey (1774 – 1843), who in turn were connected with other notable poets and authors of the time including Dorothy Wordsworth (1771 – 1855), Hartley Coleridge (1796 – 1849), Thomas de Quincey (1785 – 1859), Charles Lamb (1775 – 1834) and his sister Mary Lamb (1764 – 1847).

Along the shorelines of Grasmere and Rydal Water lie the Lakeland homes of Wordsworth and his family; Dove Cottage and Rydal Mount. Coleridge, Southey, de Quincey, John Keats, Walter Scott and Lord Byron were all drawn to the Lakes thanks to the defining work of Wordsworth, and his quietly influential sister Dorothy.

Thomas de Quincey, who was to become one of England's best known Romantic authors, moved to Rydal to be closer to Wordsworth and his stimulus. De Quincey became friendly with Peggy Simpson, whose family owned Nab Cottage, and he married her and lived with her there from 1817. Unfortunately, thanks to his towering opium addiction

understanding and appreciation of the wildlife and landscape of the Lake District as well as its potential for adventure. From a swimming perspective, both authors do us proud and express the inner child's sense of wonder and exploration. Reliving childhood dreams must be considered one of the many pleasures of adulthood and to do it whilst swimming outdoors can't be beaten.

From the stories in his books, Ransome gives us the Octopus Lagoon (Allan Tarn on the River Crake), Rio (Bowness-on-Windermere) and Wildcat Island (Peel Island on Coniston Water, see chapter 27), all wonderful places to swim in their own right, but all the more evocative if you were raised on the Swallows and Amazons stories. Beatrix Potter has given us so much more: she was a committed conservationist and was ahead of her time in recognising the problems of afforestation and the importance of biodiversity. She was the champion of our beloved Herdwick sheep and Belted Galloway cattle and invested much of her own money into land preservation and property restoration so that others could benefit from them (she left most of her land and property to the National Trust).

Potter was best known as a children's author and as a brilliant artist and illustrator (her work has been curated to good effect at The Armitt Museum in Ambleside and is worth visiting). As swimmers we can thank her for the preservation of Moss Eccles Tarn (see chapter 20) and with the places associated with her books, in particular The Tale of Squirrel Nutkin. Squirrel Nutkin is based on the adventures of the impertinent squirrel, Nutkin, and his friends who sail over to Owl Island (St Herbert's Island, Derwentwater; see chapter 8) on tiny rafts using their tails as sails. Nutkin incurs the wrath of Old Brown the owl and barely escapes minus his tail! There are few hazels on St Herberts Island these days, although I've heard an owl hunting there late at night, and the swim out to the island will forever be a favourite of mine.

and his associated debts they were forced to move out in 1833. Hartley Coleridge, the son of Samuel Taylor Coleridge moved into the cottage and remained there until his death in 1849. Mercifully, Dove Cottage, Rydal Mount and Nab Cottage have retained their original character and are very much worth visiting if only for an excuse to be close to the two most perfectly formed swimming lakes in the region: Grasmere and Rydal Water. Taken as a whole, the charming lake-filled vale and the handsome old homes of our most beloved poets and their attendant ghosts, compliment any exploration, by land or by water.

## LITERARY CONNECTIONS TO THE WATER

Adults of a certain age may have been reared on the wonderful tales of Beatrix Potter (1866 – 1943) and perhaps later on, those of Arthur Ransome (1884 – 1967) and his Swallows and Amazons adventures. Both authors display an

## ART AND WATER

As a young watercolour artist and mountaineer, I remember feeling incredibly self-conscious while attempting to capture the grandeur of Great Langdale with paint and brush, whilst perched on Raven Crag. Later on, I happened to be in Grasmere where I noticed for the first time the Heaton Cooper Gallery. Embarrassment never troubled me again and the works of William Heaton-Cooper (1903 – 1995) will remain an inspiration forever. The Heaton Cooper dynasty is as hefted to the Lakeland fells as the sheep that graze upon them. Alfred Heaton-Cooper (1863 – 1929), his son William, William's wife, the sculptor Ophelia Gordon Bell (1915 – 1975) and their son Julian Cooper (born in 1947), have all portrayed the county in their own unique styles and their work can be appreciated at their Grasmere Studio (still run by the family, Julian Cooper and Becky Heaton Cooper, William's daughter).

Although there have been many exceptional artists that have painted the Lakes, none capture the experience of being there in person and the sheer grandeur and scale of the fells, like William Heaton Cooper (except perhaps Turner). He is recognised as one of the most celebrated British landscape artists of the 20th century and was also a great writer. He produced the seminal tarn guide, The Tarns of Lakeland, which is illustrated with his wonderful watercolours and sketches; essential bedtime reading for any aspirant swim-hiker. It is apparent from his writing that the whole family were partial to a spot of mountain swimming, and he is clearly drawn to the water in all of its permutations. His depiction of water and its depth and clarity so typical of the Lake District is exceptional and as well as painting most of the tarns featured in this book, he painted all of the lakes in it too.

One cannot mention art in the Lake District and not include the talented John Ruskin (1819 – 1900). Ruskin was the leading English art critic of the Victorian era, as well as a gifted draughtsman and watercolourist. He looked to cause positive cultural and social change through his work and was considered to be an important example of a Victorian Sage (what we might now call an 'influencer'). His detailed sketches and paintings can be seen at his former home of Brantwood on Coniston. Ruskin lived at Brantwood for the last 28 years of his life and died in the Lake District in 1900. Brantwood, as well as the Ruskin Museum in Coniston are well worth a visit not just to view his artistic work; they offer a glimpse of the Lake District as it once was and a hint at what it was to become.

## HISTORY OF THE LAND

Much of the character and appearance of the Lake District countryside is far from natural; man has made his mark here since the Stone Age. Since this time the rocks and minerals hidden within the mountains have been sought after and exploited, facilitated in time by the accessible ports of the west coast. There are in excess of 300 different minerals to be found in the Lake District and lead, copper, zinc, tungsten, graphite, slate and coal are among the many that have been mined and quarried. Much of the mineral exploitation continued up until the Industrial Revolution and beyond.

Mines and slate works litter the county. Some remain valued and productive, but time has reclaimed the defunct ones, healing the scars of the past. Moss and fern have softened the edges of the spoil heaps and water has filled the old quarries, creating some fascinating places to swim (see chapter 15, for Hodge Close Quarry). Many of the water supplies that served the industrial past of the Lakes remain and also provide us with some classic swimming venues like the tarns of Potter Fell (see chapter 19), and Seathwaite Tarn in the Duddon Valley (see chapter 26). Most of them are dammed tarns and some are still used as reservoirs to supply homes and businesses today (see chapter 14 for Stickle Tarn).

During the Neolithic Period (about 4000 BC), what archaeologists refer to as the 'Langdale axe industry' was in full swing.

Tuff is a type of rock made of volcanic ash ejected from a vent during a volcanic eruption. Over time the ash is compressed by the weight of subsequent layers, turning it into a fine-grained solid rock. The quality of Langdale tuff is exceptional and the minerals present in the rock give it an attractive green colour. It was is the ideal material for making polished stone axes.

It is thought that the rock was quarried or just found as scree around the base of Harrison Stickle and Pike O' Stickle in the Langdale Valley. The relatively soft rock was then knapped into shape before being highly polished using water and softer sandstones. Polishing the rough surfaces improved the strength of the axe head and lowered friction when used to chop wood. The stone axes from Langdale are works of art as well as practical tools and have been found at archaeological sites across Britain and Ireland. It is thought that they must have been considered as objects of great value because they were traded so widely.

The traditional farming methods of Cumbria also continue to leave their mark on the land. Most of the meadows in mountainous valleys like the Duddon and Wasdale have been hard-won through the sweat and toil of generations of farmers. The vast stone mounds, or clearance cairns at Wasdale Head are testimony to their work. These mounds and much of the walling material has been hand-cleared from the ground over centuries. The grazing habits of everyone's favourite sheep, the Herdwick, have a lot to do with how our fells appear to the eye. They crop the fellside grass so short it looks like newly mowed lawn in places, anything green and succulent doesn't stand a chance of growing. Indeed, you'll often see a lone

sheep penned in local gardens to keep the lawn in order and to feed it with manure. The environment they create upon the fells is considered to be artificial by some and quintessentially Cumbrian by others – hopefully the planned rewilding of parts of the Lake District will leave room for our sheep and their bemused smiling faces, they are good company on a grim day on the fells in winter.

## EARLY EXPLORERS

Written guides to the Lake District fells are many and varied. The first, and one of the best, was Guide to the Lakes written by Wordsworth himself in 1810. The guide was initially published anonymously, was then updated and expanded over a number of editions until the sought after 1835 fifth edition was published. Guide to the Lakes is typical Wordsworth and, already recognised as a

place of beauty, drew the great and the good to the Lakes in increasing numbers.

*"The Guide is multi-faceted. It is a guide, but it is also a prose-poem about light, shapes and textures, about movement and stillness ... What holds this diversity together is the voice of complete authority, compounded from experience, intense observation, thought and love."*

- Wordsworth biographer Stephen Gill

The distinguished guidebook writer Mountford John Byrde Baddeley (1843–1906) took up the baton in 1880 when he published his Thorough Guide to the English Lake District. This became a real favourite of visitors to the Lakes in the 19th and well into the 20th century and remained in print into its 26th edition. The advice given was very general and included details of low-level walks and accom-

modation and travel advice. There were many other guidebook writers of the age of course, all with their own particular character and many of the better guides focusing on the blossoming post-war rock climbing scene led by A. Harry Griffin (1911 – 2004) and his Coniston Tigers (see The Coniston Tigers: Seventy Years of Mountain Adventure by A. Harry Griffin for more). Griffin was at heart a climber but loved to ski and swim too, sometimes in the same outing! He is probably the first person to actively seek out the Lake District tarns, swim them all and document it in his many fascinating publications. But I digress… The guidebooks scene was in Baddeley's hands for many years. Then along came A.W.

A misanthrope with a sense of humour Alfred Wainwright MBE (1907-1991) was infatuated with the Lake District and was a keen fellsman and a brilliant illustrator. From his humble, working-class background he became Britain's leading authority on fell walking in the Lakes, albeit rather reluctantly. His seven-volume Pictorial Guide to the Lakeland Fells, consisted entirely of duplications of his original hand-written volumes and was published between 1955 and 1966. Even now, 67 years after his first publication, his revised and updated guides remain the standard reference work to the 214 fells of the Lake District documented in his books. It is fair to say that amongst fellow outdoors folk he is considered a National Treasure.

The 214 fells covered in A.W.'s Pictorial Guides are considered 'Wainwrights' in his honour. They are as sought after in England as Munros are in Scotland. It is certain that Wainwright did not intend to classify the Cumbrian fells in any way, he merely detailed his favourite routes to the top of his favourite fells. But he left a legacy that many 'Wainwright Baggers' are grateful for and poring over his exquisite guidebooks prior to any fell walking adventure is considered part of the journey to the summit. The Long Distance Walker's Association (LDWA) holds a register of walkers who have successfully completed all of the Wainwrights.

*There are also 'Birketts' and 'Marilyns' in the Lake District. Wainwright didn't cover every peak in the Lake District. Birketts are based on the excellent guidebooks of local man Bill Birkett. There are 541 Birketts, many of which are also Wainwrights, they include all of the peaks within the boundary of the Lake District National Park that are over 1,000ft (305m).*

*A Marilyn is a peak with a prominence over 490ft (150m) regardless of their overall height. The list is very long at 2,011 and includes hills all over the British Isles. They were created by hillwalker and author Alan Dawson and listed in his 1992 book The Relative Hills of Britain. He named then after Marilyn Monroe. A tongue-in-cheek nod to the Munros of Scotland.*

On the ninth of July 2017, the Lake District became a UNESCO World Heritage Site, joining some of the world's most iconic locations, including Hadrian's Wall and the Taj Mahal, recognising it as a world-class cultural landscape.

The sheer scale of opportunity to engage in classic English hillwalking is overwhelming in the Lake District. This book hopes to combine some of these classic walks with equally satisfying swims and where possible, to link them to the cultural and historical character of Cumbria. Thankfully, with so much water and heritage to play with this was not too difficult a task. Since childhood I have been lucky enough to walk, climb and swim in this, the most beautiful corner of our country and trust that by sharing some of its secrets the reader will benefit from what it can give.

# THE WILD SWIMMERS CODE

To feel and be free is a wonderful thing. It is right up there with swimming, mountains and steaming mugs of tea in my list of Favourite Things. What is special about the Lake District in particular, is the freedom given to swim in vastly differing bodies of water, often situated in unspoilt and lonely locations. The accessibility to water here is unique.

With this right however, comes an absolute responsibility to follow the outdoorsman's code of leaving a place as you found it. Leaving the water as you have found it following a swim seems like a simple thing, but the increasing volume of swimmers in the Lakes is making some organisations twitchy with respect to our preferred environment. Recently, Natural England, the government's advisor for the natural environment in England, issued an edict in relation to swimming in some of our most beautiful lakes: there are to be no swimming events held in Wast Water, Buttermere, Crummock Water and Loweswater. It is unnerving that Nature England deemed it necessary to step in on our behalf to protect these lakes, in this case from the spread of non-native invasive species.

Although swimmers and swimming event organisers shouldn't shoulder the blame alone for this risk (other water users and the movements of large numbers of wildfowl also factor), we are part of a visibly growing and popular outdoor activity group. In discussions with both the National Trust (NT) and the South Cumbria Rivers Trust (SCRT) over the past 8 years, it has been evident that they

are dismayed at the potential that wild swimmers have to negatively affect the quality of our water without even realising it. In the long term the spread of certain non-native invasive species could actually impede our ability to swim in certain lakes.

I once came across Penny Webb, countryside manager for NT in the north Lakes, up to her knees in New Zealand Pygmyweed in Derwentwater attempting to clear it. Along with her team she helps to keep the spread of this very invasive species to a minimum: "The scale of the problem is big and getting worse – in recent years it's started to wrap itself around wild swimmers in the lake. The worst thing is we don't know how much there is – it's simply unmeasurable". Once it's established in a water body, it's nigh on impossible to eradicate. This is just one example of the effect of invasive species, but I'm sure you get the picture.

The adoption and promotion of a Wild Swimmers Code seems to be a prudent course of action to take. As outdoor swimmers we need to be seen to be squeaky clean and act like switched on outdoor people. An amalgamation of the "Check, Clean, Dry" campaign of the SCRT and the Countryside Code should cover it:

1. With freedom comes responsibility: respect everything and everyone, rural environments and economies are more delicate than you think. Support and help protect them.

2. Be careful where you park, camp, light a fire and how you behave.

3. Stop the Spread*: check, clean & dry equipment, clothing & dog before moving on to swim elsewhere!

4. Consider your location: is it appropriate to be swimming there? Be aware of delicate natural habitats, overuse and the location of Sites of Special Scientific Interest (SSSI)**.

*Of Non-native Invasive Species.

**SSSI's are legally protected under the Wildlife and Countryside Act 1981 and you may be liable for prosecution if you swim there.

Visit the Lakes and beyond to swim but please; love it and look after it.

# BLUE-GREEN ALGAE
# AND SWIMMING

*I*n the Lake District the presence of high concentrations of algae is a natural annual event especially in the larger lakes. These tend to be richer in nutrients which, when coupled with warm and calm weather, provide the ideal conditions for increased algal growth which often leads to the formation of algal blooms (visible as clumps and scum on the water surface). It is important to realise that the presence of blue-green algae is not a bad thing in itself. Together with other algal groups they are important contributors to the aquatic biology of fresh and marine waters. They are primary producers that:

• convert sunlight to energy by photosynthesis • release oxygen and carbon dioxide into water • take up minerals • produce food chain supporting substances

Not all blue-green algae are toxic (toxic forms are in the minority), and blue-green algae and swimming can co-exist, but there is no way to tell whether a bloom is toxic by looking at it (this requires laboratory testing). As swimmers, we must err on the side of caution and avoid areas of excessive algal blooming.

The Environment Agency is working with local businesses to reduce the levels of excessive nutrients entering the catchment area of our big Cumbria lakes. In the long term this should help to reduce the incidence of algal bloom formation.

## ALGAL BLOOMS – KEY POINTS

1. You can't tell if it's toxic, but if it looks and smells nasty, go and swim somewhere else and report it to the Environment Agency on their 24 hour hotline: 0800 80 70 60. If in doubt, stay out. Keep babies, toddlers and family pets out of the water if it looks even vaguely suspect.

2. Blanket warnings may be issued for an entire lake, even though only a small area of that lake may be affected. Use your common sense and seek out clear areas for swimming or choose another lake… we have lots of lakes, rivers and tarns that are not affected.

3. During windy weather upwind shorelines are often free of blooms, whereas downwind shores can suffer from concentrated algal blooms due to the action of the wind blowing the blooms downwind. Avoid these areas when warnings are in place.

4. If you think you may have swum through a toxic algal bloom, wash yourself off in fresh water as soon as you can and see your doctor immediately if you show any of the more serious symptoms mentioned below.

In my experience the worst symptoms that toxic blooms have caused are minor skin irritation and itchy eyes after swimming, not unlike hay fever symptoms. Hopefully following this advice will allow swimmers to make sensible decisions about where to swim during periods of suspect toxic blue-green algal blooms and to help to spread the word about suspect areas of water effectively.

# MOUNTAIN & WATER SAFETY

ell walking and outdoor swimming are not innately dangerous pastimes and most outings during a normal spring to autumn season will be nothing short of idyllic. Nevertheless, any kind of excursion into a mountain environment, particularly in the high mountains, should be treated with due respect. Outdoor swimming in remote mountain regions during the winter is inherently dangerous and should never be taken lightly, even in perfect conditions. The majority of wild swimming walks detailed in this book are not particularly extreme in any way, but most are far away from any direct form of help, often with very poor mobile phone signal. For this reason, it is important to take some simple precautions prior to any trip:

1. Research your proposed walk.
2. Check the weather for the area.
3. Dress appropriately and take the right equipment with you.
4. Take food and the means to prepare a hot drink.
5. If you are going out alone, tell someone and leave a detailed route plan.

## 1. RESEARCH YOUR PROPOSED WALK

Using a good route guide (well done, you've passed the first test) is an obvious start. Take a look at the route on a 1:25,000 Ordinance Survey map of the area detailed at the beginning of each chapter. The 1:40,000 Harvey British Mountain Maps: Lake District is also an excellent choice and covers most of the Lakes on a single map, albeit on a smaller scale.

Take the time to note the points of interest, the grid references of each swimming location and decide if you'd like to try any of the alternative route additions suggested in the route description. Although you are free to modify any of the routes in this book to your heart's content, the references included in the introduction of each chapter are there to help you get the most out of each day and provide a fast track to the interesting bits.

Finally, ask swimming friends, in person or via social media sites, for their recommendations, suggestions and advice. Most swimmers have strong opinions on where and how to swim and are usually very forthcoming with advice!

## 2. CHECK THE WEATHER FOR THE AREA

A quick check of the weather forecast on a mobile phone or online takes no time these days and can quickly help you establish the most appropriate route for the day. There are some excellent weather apps for smartphones, but we find that the MET Office app is very accurate for the Lakes. For really accurate mountain weather information the best website to use is the Mountain Weather Information Service (MWIS). The MWIS is used by mountain leaders and guides all over Britain and offers a very detailed picture of what to expect when out on the fells.

With weather, as with anything to do with personal and group safety, common sense is key. If it is blowing a gale, avoid routes on the high mountains and seek out low-level valley walks. Conversely, if it is mild and sunny, perhaps it is time to push yourself and opt for a more challenging route. Remember too, many of the remote tarn walks offer little or no shelter from the wind, so go prepared (see kit list below) or select a more weather-friendly option. Other places of interest are noted for each chapter, there is always something to do in the Lakes.

Note wind speed and direction too. Often on a very windy day good swimming can be had in the lee of the wind, using the shelter of significant land mass and forest (although it is wise to avoid forest and wooded areas in very high winds). A good example is the western shore of Windermere featured in chapters 18 and 20. This shoreline is very protected from the prevailing westerlies and can offer very satisfying swimming even in the heart of a storm.

Some of the routes in this book can become quite wild in the wind, in particular the larger lakes like Ullswater, Coniston Water, Derwentwater, Buttermere and Crummock Water. Whilst this can be exhilarating and fun for experienced swimmers, it can be daunting for the inexperienced and dramatically reduces the likelihood of ferries and power-boats being able to spot a swimmer in the water. Keep an eye out for predictions of fog and thunderstorms if you are heading out onto the big lakes too – the risk they pose is quite obvious. Avoid them.

## 3. DRESS APPROPRIATELY AND TAKE THE RIGHT EQUIPMENT WITH YOU

On average, spring and summer temperatures in the Lakes vary between 14-22°C and in winter drop as low as 4°C (and down to freezing in the high tarns). The higher you go the colder the water will be. The larger lakes tend to warm up to a surprising degree throughout the summer season and hold their warmth sometimes well into the autumn (Windermere consistently reaches over 20°C most years). Although some lakes with a north-facing catchment area like Ullswater at Glenridding, Wast Water and Buttermere can be colder by a few degrees. The rivers, becks, smaller tarns and lakes which are further up the catchment chain are more prone to cooling from freshets of rain throughout the spring summer season and of course, because of their higher altitude and tend to be much colder than the larger lakes.

Water temperatures from November through to April will be cold (between 0-10°C) and this must

be considered if you plan to try your hand at winter swimming. A remote tarn in the high fells is no place to try your first cold water swim. Play it safe; if you get into trouble there will be no one there to help you (and if there is you may be putting them at risk too if they decide to help you). Plan winter swims in the mountains carefully. Keep swims short and along the shoreline, use a tow-float and a wetsuit and neoprene accessories if you suffer from the cold. Take proper outdoor clothing that has been tried and tested and make sure you have the ability to warm up adequately afterwards with a hot brew.

'Proper outdoor clothing' means layering with efficient clothing that will insulate you, protect you from wind and rain and be able to manage the moisture from sweat you produce as you walk. Invest in good clothing and equipment and it will add to the great experience that you have planned. Here is a suggested kit list that I issue to clients before guiding them on a wild swimming walk:

• Swimwear, swim cap and goggles (good for trout watching in river pools)
• Wetsuit or neoprene top
• High visibility tow float (essential for the larger lakes and remote tarns)
• Pack towel or lightweight changing robe
• Waterproofs, outdoor clothing including baselayer (Merino wool baselayers are recommended), spare fleece, warm woollen socks and boots
• Warm hat and gloves and/or sunhat, insect

repellent and sunscreen depending on the forecast
- A comfortable rucksack large enough to carry your kit in with a dry bag liner (30-40 litres in size should cover every eventuality)
- Packed lunch, snacks, drink and a sit mat
- Flask of hot drink, or a lightweight brew kit (stove, gas, pot and tea)
- Water or water filter/purification tablets
- Small waterproof drybag for phone and keys
- Trekking poles, if you use them
- Lots of cash for car parking (many Lakes car parks are expensive and only take cash)
- Compact First Aid Kit

In the colder months, or early and late in the season, I would add a group shelter or a tarp to this list as well as a down or insulated jacket. They can be invaluable in providing shelter and help with warming up post-swim. If you plan to use a group shelter or tarp, familiarise yourself with them first, there are plenty of good YouTube tutorials of how to use them.

Even during windy days during the summer, a bit of shelter can make the difference between an enjoyable day out and one to simply endure. With experience you should be able to work out the best kit to take along for you and your group without being overburdened with gear.

## 4. TAKE FOOD AND THE MEANS TO PREPARE A HOT DRINK

Eating and drinking are one of the best ways to warm up post-swim; they cause an increase in body temperature thanks to dietary thermogenesis. Aside from warming you up, what is better than a picnic and a nice cuppa next to your favourite tarn or river pool?

Swimmers seldom need advice on the kinds of yummy food you can take for post-swim nourishment, so I'll keep it short:

Take a packed lunch and generous amounts of chocolate and/or cake. A flask or a brew kit will complement your picnic and a means of purifying water will save you having to lug about huge water bottles. There are some excellent water filters available from outdoor suppliers these days, most of which are incorporated into lightweight bottles or bladders. They allow you to quickly purify river, lake and tarn water for drinking.

## 5. IF YOU ARE GOING OUT ALONE, TELL SOMEONE AND LEAVE A DETAILED ROUTE PLAN

Solo travel is often frowned on as irresponsible, in particular if you are swimming alone too. As long as common sense is applied at all times then going it alone is perfectly safe and a bit of solitude and peace isn't going to hurt anyone.

However, it is standard practice to take a few precautions, just in case you end up with a twisted ankle beside a remote and seldom visited tarn with no mobile phone signal.

Tell someone what your plans are and leave them with a detailed route plan, including timings and when you plan to return. Leave a copy of this route plan in a waterproof bag tucked under your windscreen wiper too if you have arrived by car. Outdoor folk, and mountain rescue team members get very nervous when they see cars that have been abandoned in car parks overnight. A quick explanatory note detailing your route, what you plan to do and at what time, and what time you should be back can ease any concerns or help effect a quick rescue if you need it.

For many of the popular routes during the busy summer season, this precaution may be overkill, but some of the routes detailed in this book do go off the grid and can be quite remote. Seldom have I met anyone en route to Codale Tarn (see chapter 16) or Scoat and Low Tarn (see chapter 22) for example, even during the high season. Play it safe, go prepared, have a great time and return with a smile on your face to tell the tale.

# GETTING THERE

## BY CAR

Travelling by car offers the most scope for flexibility within the Lakes but parking can be a problem during the holiday seasons. See the Lake District National Park (LDNP) website for information on car parks and 'park and explore' tickets which cover a day's parking and bus travel across the Lake District.

Electric car hire is available within the National Park at railway station locations, see zap-map.com for locations, types and prices of charge points and their useful journey planner to calculate distances and costs. Electric cars are a very sustainable way to get around the Lakes and there are lots of charging points across the region to facilitate this.

The M6 runs to the east of the Lake District National Park. Junction 36 leads to the A590 for the southern end of the Lake District, Junction 40 and the A66 or A592 leads to the northern end of the Lake District. Beware of relying solely on sat nav to get to where you want to go, they are not always reliable on our small country roads.

## BY TRAIN

The West Coast mainline runs to the east of the Lake District, connecting Oxenholme, Penrith and Carlisle with London and Glasgow. A direct train runs from Manchester to Windermere. Local trains call at Kendal, Staveley and Windermere.

## BY BUS

National Express run coaches to various towns in the Lake District from all over the UK. Most of the Lakes is well-serviced by local bus services which link to the major rail and bus stations with the exception of specific, more remote locations. These are: Mardale (Route 6), Swindale (Route 7), Mosedale (Route 1), Eskdale (Routes 24 & 25), Dunnerdale (Route 26) and Wasdale (Routes 22 & 23).

## BY BOAT

Windermere, Ullswater, Coniston and Derwentwater have passenger boats with multiple stops. The LDNP website has information on stops, timetables, and links to supplier websites.

## BY AIR

The nearest airports are Manchester to the south and Glasgow to the north. There is a railway station at Manchester airport with services that run to Oxenholme next to Kendal, Staveley and Windermere.

Carlisle Lake District Airport is now open, offering flights from Dublin, Belfast and London Southend.

*Walk 1*

# RIVER CALDEW AND BOWSCALE TARN

A lovely circular walk along the River Caldew with its shimmering river pools followed by the Quest for the immortal talking fish of Bowscale Tarn.

## INFORMATION

DISTANCE: 7.1 miles

TIME: 4 hours

MAP: Harvey British Mountain Map: Lake District, OS Explorer OL5 The English Lakes NE

START/END POINT: Mosedale Village (NY 356 322)

SWIMMING: River Caldew (NY 327 326), Bowscale Tarn (NY 336 313)

PARKING: Park considerately for free near Mosedale Bridge, or in the Mosedale Quaker Meeting House Car Park (£2 donation requested).

PUBLIC TRANSPORT: The nearest train station is Penrith. Stagecoach buses X5 and X50 run regularly between Penrith and Keswick. The nearest stop is "Mungrisdale Road Ends" which is a few miles away from Mosedale. The 'Caldbeck Rambler' 73/73a operates an infrequent return service from Carlisle through Mungrisdale to Keswick.

PLACES OF INTEREST: Grainsgill Beck Mines – remains of early 19th century tungsten mill and workings, Celtic hill fort, Mosedale Quaker Meeting House.

REFRESHMENTS: Mosedale Friends Meeting House Café, Mosedale (CA11 0XQ); The Mill Inn, Mungrisdale, serves good food and ale (017687 79632, CA11 0XR).

ACCOMMODATION: Mosedale End Farm Bed and Breakfast & Glamping Pod, Mosedale (07917 050893, Penrith CA11 0XQ); Mosedale House, Mosedale, offers self-catering accommodation (017687 79371, Penrith CA11 0XQ); The Mill Inn, Mungrisdale is a 17th century coaching inn which serves good food and ale (017687 79632, CA11 0XR).

To look down the Caldew Valley from Mosedale always brings peace of mind. Knowing that the level road ahead leads into one of the quieter parts of the Lakes and that it is bordered all along by the shimmering Caldew River, is balm for the soul. As road walks go, this is one is very enjoyable. Mosedale itself is peaceful and unspoilt, a suitable location for one of the earliest Quaker meeting houses in Cumbria (built in 1702), with associations to George Fox who founded the Quakers. The house is open to visitors during the summer months and is well worth a visit for the opportunity for quiet contemplation and the company of like-minded others.

This valley gives access to the fells at the 'Back O Skidda' and the keen fell walker could entertain themselves here for a lifetime. However, the swim hiker will be drawn inevitably to Bowscale Tarn ❹ via the pools and falls of the river beneath. Don't be in too much of a rush to get to the tarn though, there are enough delightful little river pools to fill a day along the valley. The last time I visited in the early summer, the pools were stuffed with small brown trout and the entire day was spent admiring their black and buttery, crimson spotted forms.

The road runs right beside the river from the Roundhouse, a former farmhouse and barn, and it is from here onwards that the best of the pools can be found. After about 3 kilometres of walking the road becomes more track and heads south-west at the base of one of the extended spurs of Knott. Continuing north for a short way at this point leads you up Grainsgill Beck to some old mine workings and the remains of an early 20th century tungsten mill. Interesting features to be found here include adits (tunnels), stopes (large underground rooms), open cuts, shafts,

In his poem 'Song at the Feast of Brougham Castle', Wordsworth celebrates the restoration of the 'Shepherd Lord', Henry Clifford to the Estates and Honours of his Ancestors. Henry was sent away by his mother to protect him during the War of the Roses, to live a shepherd's life. Local legend had it that he was at one with the local fauna and was on speaking terms with the fish of Bowscale Tarn. Later in life he was to become one of the most powerful lords in the North.

spoil heaps, machine beds, trackways and a ruined dam at Brandy Gill.

The Cumbria Way follows the River Caldew at an acute south-westerly angle from the small bridge spanning Grainsgill Beck. This leads to a sheepfold where Long and Short Gill can be seen to carve into the flanks of Bowscale Fell. The ascent of the spur between the two gills, gives a rapid route to the summit, relative to individual fitness levels! The views of the valley beneath are, as ever, worth the effort and the prospect of a swim in the tarn ahead is something to rightfully look forward to.

Dropping off Bowscale Fell and skirting the western edge of Tarn Crags before contouring into the corrie, brings you to Bowscale Tarn nestled in its north-facing, craggy corrie and hemmed in by whale-backed moraine. This was a popular tourist attraction in Victorian times when visitors could enjoy a pony ride to the tarn to observe its wild and moody aspect. The tarn is associated with the legend of two immortal fish who could speak – a legend that was popularised by our very own William Wordsworth and then no doubt expanded upon by the travel writers of the time, one of whom (Eliza Lynn Linton, a local Keswick lass) even provided the names of the fish: Adam and Eve.

*To his side the fallow-deer*
*Came and rested without fear;*
*The eagle, lord of land and sea,*
*Stooped down to pay him fealty;*
*And both the undying fish that swim*
*Through Bowscale-tarn did wait on him;*
*The pair were servants of his eye*
*In their immortality;*
*And glancing, gleaming, dark or bright,*
*Moved to and fro, for his delight.*

Being a north-facing corrie tarn, Bowscale can be on the chilly side when it comes to swimming, but it never disappoints and the legend, however fantastical, always prompts me to peer into the gloomy depths with my goggles on, looking for the dull glint of scales.

The return journey, which follows the old pony route, gives more great views of the valley along with a respect for the industrious Victorian guides and their no doubt, long-suffering ponies. On arrival at Bowscale, it is a mere half mile to Mosedale and perhaps a cup of tea and homemade cake in the Garth at the Mosedale Friends Meeting House if they are open and serving as they usually are throughout the season.

**1** Follow the road west from the Quaker Meeting House in Mosedale until you see the river that runs by the road. Continue on, exploring the river pools until you reach the small bridge at Grainsgill Beck. If time or inclination allow head north-west here taking the obvious, signposted track, to explore the mine workings above.
**1.9 miles**

**2** From the bridge, continue along the dwindling track south-west for 500 metres until you see the sheepfold by the river. Ford the river and head up to the right of Short Gill where the fell is less steep. Cross Long Gill further up (about 50 metres up from the confluence of the two gills) and continue on up the low spur that soon flattens out and leads steadily to Bowscale Fell summit at 702 metres.
**1.9 miles**

**3** At the summit, follow the broad ridgeline north-east for about 300 metres before following the easier ground that forms a ridge and skirts Tarn Crags. Continue the descent until it is possible to follow a path to contour into the corrie at an acute angle, south, south-east. Follow the well-worn path to the tarn.
**1.2 miles**

**4** The descent home takes the rambling pony track that in most part, follows the contours of the fell making it fairly easy on the legs. Follow the obvious path north and onwards as it gradually takes the path of least resistance, heading east back towards civilization at Bowscale village. When you arrive at the road at Bowscale turn left and follow the road back to Mosedale via the bridge.
**2.1 miles**

# Walk 2

# SILVER BAY AND
# THE ULLSWATER ISLANDS

An exciting walk out, swim back, island-hopping adventure, taking in the best of the Ullswater islands including Norfolk Island, Lingy Holme and the Devil's Chimney.

I t is worth pointing out early on, that when the swimming begins on this route you will need to pack everything you are wearing and carrying into your tow float and then swim with it. If you have never done this before, please practice before you begin. My advice would be to pack light, keep an eye on the forecast, choosing a nice day, and have a large breakfast so you don't need to pack much food! Either that or take someone along who doesn't swim to support you.

Ullswater is one of the most attractive big lakes in the Lake District and mercifully, maintains a genteel atmosphere sometimes lacking in other parts of the Lakes. This southernmost end of the lake is the most dramatic and is surrounded by classic hill walking fells: to the west lies Sheffield Pike, Birkhouse Moor and the massif of Helvellyn beyond, to the south St Sunday Crag and the foothills of Fairfield. The east is dominated by Place Fell and Patterdale Common with the heights of High Street lying beyond. The fell walking from Patterdale and along the eastern shoreline follows the low lying contours of Patterdale Common and the walking is easy going with spectacular views to the south and west. It also allows a good view of the swimming to come, and it is interesting to see and experience this route from two very different perspectives.

The water here can be very cool, relative to the other large lakes in the region, due in no small part to the north-facing catchment area flowing into Ullswater from Goldrill, Deepdale, Grisedale and Glenridding Becks. But of course, the swimming is sublime and on a calm sunny day there is no better place to be in the Lakes. However, the canny outdoor swimmer will keep an eye on the weather, and in particular the wind speed and direction prior

## INFORMATION

DISTANCE: Walking distance 3.5 miles, swimming distance about 1.1 miles (if you follow the shoreline and swim to Norfolk Island)
TIME: About 2.5 hours walking, 1 hour swimming. Account for slower swim speed when towing a loaded tow float.
MAP: Harvey British Mountain Map: Lake District, OS Explorer OL5 The English Lakes NE
START/END POINT: Patterdale Hotel Car Park (NY 395 159, CA11 0NW)
PUBLIC TRANSPORT: The 508 runs from Penrith to Patterdale. During holidays and weekends the 208 also stops in Patterdale. A company called Co-wheels offers hire cars based next to train stations at Oxenholme, Windermere and Penrith for short or long term hire.
SWIMMING: Ullswater (NY 397 184), visiting the islands and bays along the way.
PARKING: Pay and display car park opposite the Patterdale Hotel. If this is full then you may need to find parking in Glenridding and walk back to the start of the walk.
PLACES OF INTEREST: Artists' Seat, Silver Crag, Devil's Chimney, Aira Force waterfall
REFRESHMENTS: The White Lion Inn, great 19th century inn, Patterdale (017684 82214, CA11 0NW); Patterdale Hotel, Patterdale, (017684 82231, CA11 0NN); Old Water View Hotel, Patterdale, (017684 82175, CA11 0NW)

to swimming. When the wind blows hard from the south or west it can become ferocious as it is funnelled down onto the water by the shape of the surrounding fells and can whip up some very challenging swimming conditions. This can provide exciting swimming for the strong and experienced swimmer but is not for the fainthearted.

Ullswater has some interesting history, and there are two men who will forever be associated with it, namely Lord Birkett and Donald Campbell.

Lord Birkett did us all a great service by helping to revoke a Bill in the House of Lords which would have allowed the lake to be used as a reservoir, which would have dramatically restricted its use for recreational purposes. There is a plaque dedicated to him on the face of Kailpot Crag and a carved stone memorial dedicated to him at Pooley Bridge.

Donald Campbell not only broke the World Water Speed Record here in 1955, but he also broke the 200mph barrier on water. This was a remarkable achievement at the time and adds to the fascinating heritage associated with the lake. There is a slate memorial dedicated to Campbell at Glenridding Pier and the golden days of speedboating in the Lakes is now over. Bad news for speed demons, but great news for swimmers. The 10 mph speed limit reduces the risk from powerboats, but the lake

can get very busy at times, and it pays to remain up to date with the Ullswater Steamer timetable and perhaps notify them of your intentions if you are planning to swim during the busy summer season. You can call into the office at Glenridding Pier or contact them using the details on their website.

The walk up to Silver Crag is a joy as is the crag itself. It bristles with heather, rowan and holly, and bilberry and juniper are rampant. Of course, it is well worth exploring if only for the lake views and it is fun to follow the winding tracks through the vicious juniper bushes. There is a tiny tarn on the small col that separates Birk Fell from the crag that must be the loveliest piece of un-swimmable water I know of. It is miniature perfection, and always makes me smile when I pass it by.

Once in the water at Silver Bay **3a**, you are in for a real swimming treat, no matter how many times I swim from here it always feels like an adventure. Running the gauntlet from Silver Point to Norfolk Island and back should give you a taste of what is ahead. Play it safe when crossing here. It is the only point during the swim that you will potentially put yourself directly in the path of the Ullswater Steamers and other pleasure craft. There is no shame in missing this crossing out on a busy day and sticking to contouring the fascinating shoreline. Lingy Holm provides a welcome place to scan the route ahead and to pick out the crag that holds Devil's Chimney. On a warm summer day, it is also an excellent place just to loll about and soak up the warmth – you will almost certainly have it all to yourself.

The swimming route for this journey takes us right to the foot of Devil's Chimney **4**, a dark and gloomy, non-descript cliff, plunging direct and deep into the lake beneath. If you are early enough and catch the mist on the water on an early autumn morning, you might witness the phenomenon that gives the place its name: mist swirling off the water and up the black chimney fault line, like smoke coming up from hell! The views from this point are far from hellish however, and the little wooded outcrop is the ideal place for a picnic and to take some photographs. It is hard to leave the sheltered comfort and beauty of this place, but the walk ahead is pleasant and something to look forward to and the prospect of a nice drink on the lawn of the Patterdale Hotel gives a spring to the step.

*Distance swimmers may be drawn to continue their swim further south, past Purse Point and the lovely Blowick Bay, and on towards the western shore and Glenridding Pier. This is an exciting option and provides some excellent swimming, but really puts you in the firing line of other lake users. So, if you do go for it, go in a group, stay switched on and don't take unnecessary risks. Please note that the rest of the eastern shoreline of Ullswater, south of Devil's Chimney is private and is not an appropriate exit point for swimmers.*

*If you are staying at Side Farm Campsite, you could extend the swimming route all the way down to the campsite, passing Purse Point and Blowick Bay en route. The campsite borders the lake giving you good access, as well as warm showers post-swim.*

## WEEKEND SUGGESTION

Stay in Patterdale and take this swim hike once you have recovered from your journey; it is not too much of an epic and will give you a taste for a bigger challenge the following day. Choose from the Helvellyn swim hike and look forward to swimming in lofty Red Tarn or really treat yourself to a big day out and head off for the Hartsop Tarns walk.

**1** From the Patterdale Hotel Car Park follow the road north-west towards Glenridding for 200 metres where you will see the right of way on the right side of the road, next to the George Starkey Climber's Hut. Follow this over the bridge which crosses Goldrill Beck until you come to Side Farm. Turn left here onto the bridleway that takes you along to the farm campsite about 600 metres ahead. Continue past the moss-covered barn next to the track until you come to Artist's Seat, dedicated to Turner, Macbeth and Glover.
**1.1 miles**

**2** From the Artists' Seat head north-east up the grass path to the obvious spinney of larch, sycamore, and oak. Stay on the indistinct footpath that follows the

wall for about 150 metres until the path bears uphill to join the large bridleway track. Carry on the bridleway, bordered by hawthorn and holly, as you gradually ascend towards the small col and Silver Crag above. Stop and explore awhile as the views from the crag are worth the short, steep hike to the top.

Once the exploration of Silver Crag has been completed, continue north past the lovely tarnlet, and make the descent down the rocky track to Silver Bay which is clearly visible ahead. Turn left at the main path then right after about 10 meters, heading towards the large ash tree. From here an indistinct trod follows the gill down to Silver Bay.
**0.8 miles**

**3a** Now the swimming begins. Keeping 30 metres or so from the shoreline, swim west (to the left) around Silver Point until you are exactly opposite Norfolk Island. Take a good look around for approaching boats and if you deem it safe to do so, take a direct line toward the island. The swim across is only 200 metres or so but it feels very exposed and is an exhilarating swim if there is a bit of chop. Take a tour of the island and its little satellites and head back the way you came, taking the same precautions.

Follow the shoreline south to the welcome haven of Lingy Holm, a low, rocky island which can provide some nice shelter if there is a breeze from the south-west. From Lingy Holme continue to

follow the shore, heading towards the dark crag of Devil's Chimney which forms a blunt promontory out into the lake. Just past Devil's Chimney, you will see the wall that comes down to the shore and a tiny pebble beach; this is the exit point of the swim. Here a worn path leads steeply up by the wall then heads left towards a large old larch guarded by towering oaks. Continue on into atmospheric, mixed woodland and more level ground.
**1.1 miles**

**3b** The non-swimmer or support crew can enjoy the walk to Devil's Chimney whilst keeping an eye on your swimmer(s) en route. From Silver Bay retrace your steps back to the main bridleway which heads west before following the shoreline south almost directly to the plantation which precedes the Devil's Chimney. Don't head off too fast though, a path pulls away from the bridleway just along from the bay that leads all the way to Silver Point which gives an ideal vantage point to observe your swimmer(s) heading out to Norfolk Island.

Back on the bridleway, head south and continue the steady ascent to the plantation. At the top turn right and down through mixed woodland towards the lake, remembering to stop before you fall down Devil's Chimney itself. You can use the wall at the northernmost end of the plantation as a handrail if you are uncertain of the direction to take, as there are many confused tracks. This wall will lead you directly to the swim exit point.
**0.6 miles**

**4** From Devil's Chimney head up through the plantation heading east (or follow the exit wall) until you get back to the bridleway. Follow this south for about 500

metres until you reach the Artists' Seat then on toward Side Farm to eventually take the right turn that will take you back over the Goldrill Beck to Patterdale.
**1.6 miles**

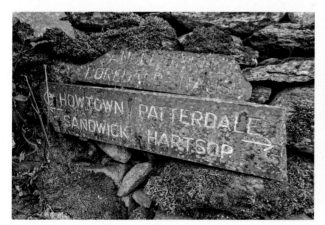

# Walk 3

# HOWTOWN, SANDWICK AND KAILPOT CRAG

A lovely, manageable, and classic walk from Howtown which features swimming from Sandwick Bay and Kailpot Crag, via one of the best woodland walks in Lakeland.

Y ou can get to the beginning of this swim hike in several ways: Either take the lovely drive around to Howtown via Pooley Bridge along the side of the lake and hope to find somewhere to park. Alternatively get the bus to Pooley Bridge and walk to Howtown which is a bit of a hike. Taking the Ullswater Steamer from Glenridding to Howtown provides the most exciting option, however they only do one way tickets, so you are not guaranteed a return journey (you can sometimes board at Howtown if they have room for you). Which in my opinion makes it even more fun (but not everyone may agree)?

No matter how you get to Howtown, you will be taken by the pleasantly remote feeling of this quaint hamlet perched on the edge of Ullswater. There is not much there aside from the wonderful Howtown Hotel and the famous Outward Bound Education Centre, but of course, this is part of its charm. The name Howtown Wyke is a nice combination of Old English and Old Norse. Howtown meaning 'settlement by the hill' and Wyke meaning an inlet or bay. It is a wonderful place from which to explore the relatively quiet surrounding fells and of course, the shores of Ullswater.

This route takes you around the diminutive, but perfectly formed Hallin Fell. Hallin Fell is classified as a Marilyn, meaning it has a prominence of 150 metres, and presents itself as an independent little mountain from most angles. The views from the summit are great but we will stick to circumnavigating its base on this route and leave the climbing to another day.

The walk from the pier at Howtown Wyke takes you south and briefly into Fusedale, skirting the ridge of Steel Knotts, past the Coombs and onwards, following the path of Sandwick Beck.

## INFORMATION

DISTANCE: 3.75 miles
TIME: 3.5 hours
MAP: Harvey British Mountain Map: Lake District, OS Explorer OL5 The English Lakes NE
START/END POINT: Howtown Wyke Pier (NY 443 199)
PUBLIC TRANSPORT: The nearest train station is Penrith. The Stagecoach 508 bus service runs from Penrith to Pooley Bridge
SWIMMING: Sandwick Bay (NY 426 200), Kailpot Crag (NY 433 204)
PLACES OF INTEREST: Aira Force waterfall (NY 401 201, CA11 0JY), Ullswater Steamers (017684 82229, CA11 0US)
REFRESHMENTS: The Howtown Hotel, Howtown (01768 486514, CA10 2ND,)
NEARBY SWIM SPOTS: Any accessible shore on Ullswater will provide a fine swimming location, Silver Bay and the islands are a good place to start. The tarns of Patterdale and Hartsop offer a good day out.

*The air is full of a farewell –*
*Deserted by the silver lake*
*Lies the wide world, overturned.*
*Cities rise where mountains fell,*
*The furnace where the phoenix burned.*

*On Leaving Ullswater* - Kathleen Raine

The walking can be rough at times but is fairly easy-going if you have come prepared and are used to it. It is a treat to be so immediately immersed in the fells with the prospect of the wonderful lake views just around the corner.

It is worth popping into the 'new' Martindale church of St. Peter just after the Coombs. It was built in the 1880s and stands atop Martindale Hause, featuring some very fine and wonderfully colourful stained glass work by Jane Grey, the famed British stained glass artist. The 'old' church lies half a mile south of the new, further up the valley and is dedicated to St Martin of Tours. The present building dates from the 16th century but the first reference to a church being here was in 1220. On the grounds you encounter a stunning 1,300-year-old yew tree.

The highlight of the walk is through Hallinhag Wood ❸ and it is worth taking your time in these delightful woods. Explore the shoreline where possible; there are myriad opportunities to swim here, from the bay all the way to Kailpot Crag. Keep an eye out for The Poetry Stones in the wood, they are hard to spot until you get your eye in. They celebrate the poetry of Kathleen Raine, who moved to the valley as an evacuee with her family during WW2, they offer the adventurer a moment to think, and give an insight into the solace that this beautiful place gave to many during the war.

Kailpot Crag ❹ must, of course, be singled out for its jumping off potential. You must do it, or you don't get the full tick for the route. Many a happy hour can be spent here, just messing about in the water and heckling your friends and family while they are poised for the jump. The crag also provides a great viewpoint from which to admire Ullswater. You can thank Lord Birket, whose commemorative plaque you have been jumping over, for your access to it. The lakeside plaque was dedicated by the Bishop of Penrith to the man "by whose vision and labours the values of this beautiful spot were discerned, defined and defended to the common welfare of all who seek here refreshment of body, mind and spirit." Amen to that.

In the early 1960s the Manchester Corporation planned to use the lake as a reservoir which would have effectively restricted recreational use, and a Bill went to the House of Lords. Lord Birkett, who was considered to be a superb advocate and judge, apparently made the greatest speech of his life when he spoke against the Bill. He outlined the importance of retaining Ullswater's natural beauty for all to enjoy. Thankfully the Bill was repealed but tragically, while enjoying congratulations from his peers the following day, Birket's health deteriorated rapidly, and he died shortly afterwards.

The walk from Kailpot around Geordie's Crag provides more expansive lake views and leads you gently back to Howtown Wyke via Waternook.

**1** From the pier at Howtown Wyke head east along the shoreline path for about 50m to the road that leads into Howtown. Turn right and walk along the road for about 100m meters and take the bridleway south between the walls towards the buildings ahead. Pass between the buildings and carry on along the rack that heads south and which eventually leads on towards Fusedale. About 200m on from the buildings take the track heading west, which skirts the base of Steel End ridge. Follow the track which crosses the Coombs for 800m, here the track forks, take the left fork which leads to Lanty's Tarn. From the tarn, follow the track heading north which soon leads to St. Peter's Church.

**1 mile**

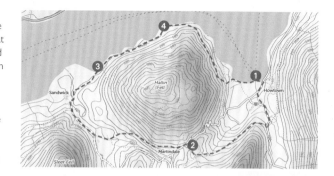

**2** From St. Peter's Church continue north on the track to the road which ascends Martindale Hause and follow the steep road south-west for about 100m and take the footpath on the right, heading due west, which traverses the meadows of Hause Farm. At the final wall, cross the footpath and carry on following the westward path which heads towards Hallin Bank. Keep heading west through the walls at Hallin Bank and continue on towards Bridge End and Howegrain Beck. Cross the beck at the bridge and turn right onto the track that continues west and on over Boredale Beck.

Turn right onto the road heading north-west and follow this all the way to Beckside Farm at Sandwick.

At the end of the road, a track leads north-east and over Sandwick Beck. This track follows the beck, then the north-east trending wall, and soon leaves Hallinhag Wood and Sandwick Bay. You can swim from here as the shoreside path gives good access to Sandwick Bay.

**1.25 miles**

**3** From Sandwick Bay follow the path north east all the way to the northern most end of the Hallinhag Wood (remembering to look out for the Poetry Stones).

After 900m meters of walking, the footpath emerges from the woods

and immediately on the left and to the north, lies the promontory that houses Kailpot Crag. Remember to take care and check for obstructions before jumping.

**0.5 miles**

**4** From Kailpot Crag, head east towards Geordie's Crag and follow the path all the way around, as it bears around to the south, south east, to Waternook, a distance of about 1km. Just past the buildings at Waternook, the path reaches the wall. Carry on through the gate in the wall and follow the track that leads to the lake shore path to Howtown Wyke.

**0.8 miles**

# Walk 4

# HELVELLYN, RED TARN, GLENRIDDING BECK AND ULLSWATER

A classic hill walk and a big day out. Swimming in Red Tarn, Glenridding Beck and Ullswater offers every kind of mountain swimming experience.

The Helvellyn massive has probably inspired more adventure than any other area in the Lakes and is the largest single mass of high ground in the region. At 950 metres it is the third highest peak in the Lake District and Helvellyn itself is the most prominent point on the great ridgeline of fells that joins north to south. The variety of mountain terrain to be found here attracts climbers, mountaineers, hill walkers, skiers and adventurous swimmers and its popularity is only heightened by its accessibility. The weather on the fell here can be changeable and fierce, providing a real challenge to endurance and navigation, but the short, sharp descent routes to the west, or the sinuous ridgelines and hidden coves to the east offer relatively quick passage to safety. For the canny adventurer it provides a veritable playground, rich in history and with enough lonely corners away from the beaten track to satisfy the craving for wilderness.

As Heaton Cooper notes in his *The Tarns of Lakeland*, it is evident to all with a basic understanding of geography that this is a landscape carved by glacial action on a massive scale and that the Helvellyn corrie that hold Red Tarn must have been one of the last strongholds of the ice. The awesome eroding power of the glaciation that occurred here is very evident when stood on the edge of the tarn, dressed only in swimming trunks, gazing up at the 800 foot back wall of the corrie and the encircling arêtes of Striding and Swirral Edge. The tarn is the highest and smallest lake to contain the rare and protected schelly, a type of freshwater herring left over from the ice age. It is relatively rich in life considering its location, also containing a good head of brightly speckled brown trout.

## INFORMATION

DISTANCE: 8.4 miles
TIME: 6 hours
MAP: Harvey Maps: Lake District BMC (British Mountain Maps), OS Explorer OL5 The English Lakes NE
START/END POINT: Glenridding Car Park (NY 385 169, CA11 0PA).
PUBLIC TRANSPORT: Penrith is the nearest train station. Glenridding is served by buses 108 from Penrith and 508 to Penrith. You can also get to Glenridding by lake steamer from Pooley Bridge and Howtown.
SWIMMING: Red Tarn (NY 350 153), Glenridding Beck (NY 371 172), Ullswater (NY 390 170)
PLACES OF INTEREST: Aira Force waterfall (NY 401 201, CA11 0JY), Ullswater Steamers (017684 82229, CA11 0US), Greenside Lead Mine (CA11 0QR, NY 363 174)
REFRESHMENTS: The Travellers Rest is a great pub on the descent route (017684 82298, CA11 0QQ). The Glenridding Hotel, Beckside Bar and Bistro offers good pub food (017684 82228, CA11 0PB). Fellbites Café Restaurant is right next to the car park (017684 82781, CA11 0PD). R and R Corner Shop offers a good selection of takeaway hot drinks and snacks (07928 792565, CA11 0PA).
EASIER ACCESS: Good level access to Ullswater from Glenridding Pier Car Park.
NEARBY SWIM SPOTS: Silver Bay and the Ullswater Islands are a short walk from Glenridding. The tarns of Patterdale and Hartsop offer a good day out further up the valley.

Helvellyn has been a popular destination for visitors to the Lake District since the late 18th century and was mentioned in the earliest guidebooks on the region. Samuel Taylor Coleridge and Wordsworth enjoyed walks here and the good old Victorians even enjoyed pony rides to the summit, via the zig-zag route up Whiteside. As a dramatic and popular mountain, with so many different routes to the top, it has many stories to tell.

On the path leading from Striding Edge to the summit plateau, lies the Gough Memorial, erected in 1890. Charles Gough was a headstrong young Quaker and aspiring romantic artist, visiting the Lake District as a tourist. In April 1805 he headed off to climb Striding Edge with his faithful spaniel, Foxie, with the hope of capturing the dramatic atmosphere of Helvellyn on canvas. Alas, he fell to his death and was discovered by a shepherd three months later, a mere skeleton, with his hat split in two and Foxie still standing faithfully by her master's side.

The fact that Foxie looked remarkably well fed was subsequently glossed over and both William Wordsworth and Sir Walter Scott wrote poems about the tragedy and romanticised depictions of the scene were painted by Francis Danby and Edwin Landseer (the reality of the scene must have been much more macabre!).

*Dark green was that spot 'mid the*
*brownmountain heather,*
*Where the pilgrim of nature lay stretched in decay,*
*Like the corpse of an outcast abandoned to weather,*
*Till the mountain-winds wasted the tenantless clay.*

From *Helvellyn* - Sir Walter Scott

A further tragedy was that Gough gained fame at the expense of his own death and became an icon of the romantic ideal. He was buried in the Quaker graveyard at Tirril, near Penrith.

The following century, things had moved on somewhat, but young men were still apt to do silly things on mountains. About 35 meters south of the summit shelter lies a small stone tablet commemorating the first plane ever to have landed on a mountain top. This was during the 1920s and the purpose of the brave stunt was to prove the capability of modern aircraft, showing off their ability to land in the most improbable of places. After two previously aborted attempts Bert Hinkler, a test pilot who worked for A V Roe, the plane's manufacturers, and John F. Leeming, president of the Lancashire Aero Club, successfully landed their Avro 585 Gosport two-seater biplane on the rock-strewn summit plateau on 22 December 1926.

Apparently, the landing was a breeze – the steep slope and strong headwind helped to slow the plane quite effectively. The uphill take-off was a bit hairier as the reverse was true and the plane dived off the plateau, narrowly missing Striding Edge before the relieved crew headed home to Woodford Aerodrome near Manchester.

Not all pilots were so lucky. On 10 February 1945 Warrant Officer William G D Frost (pilot) and Flight Sergeant Corbie F Marshall (navigator) took off from RAF Cranfield in Bedfordshire for a night exercise in their de Havilland Mosquito. They both died when they hit the summit of Catstycam and crashed into Striding Edge while attempting to assess their position in low cloud. The wreckage of the aircraft fell down the crags and onto Red Tarn, which was covered in thick ice at the time. After the remains of the crew were recovered the airplane wreckage was left to sink through the ice in the spring. In May 2004, 60 years after the crash, the wreckage was recovered

from the tarn by divers for photographing and study before being returned to the deeps.

The ascent of Birkhouse Moor ❷ en route to Red Tarn is steep and unforgiving, but the route offers some excellent views across the surrounding fells and Ullswater. Once the height is gained the walker can look forward to an almost level path past the 'Hole-in-the-Wall' and on to Striding Edge. Described by Wainwright as, "The best way of all [to the summit] ... The big attraction is an airy rock ridge, very fine indeed. Good path throughout." Take great care in high wind or icy conditions but otherwise walk boldly on and enjoy it for what it is: the finest ridge walk in the Lakes.

The summit plateau is rather exposed and can be an eerie place in fog, with only the stone shelter, located some way from the summit cairn, for protection. On a good day the views are spellbinding and the prospect of the descent down Swirral Edge ❸ to the north-east, seen in its full glory sweeping dramatically towards Catstycam with Red Tarn beneath is a thrilling prospect. Swirrel, a dialect variation of swirl can mean 'giddiness' as well as being used to describe a place on the fells where wind or snow swirls around. Both meanings are apt regarding the description of this stunning arête, which drops steeply in a series of stone steps and blocks from the Helvellyn plateau, leading the way along the ridge and then down towards the tarn.

Red Tarn ❹ fills almost the entire base of the cirque and is the highest substantial body of water in England according to the Brathay Exploration Group and at 718 metres above sea level it is the sixth highest tarn in the Lake District. It is retained by the terminal moraine through which Red Tarn Beck makes its escape, to tumble down to Glenridding below and its cold, slate green waters make for one of the finest swimming spots in the

Lake District. Striking out across the tarn in the shadow of the crags on a wild mountain day, with the weather swirling above and whipping the water into spume, is an experience never to be forgotten.

The path to Glenridding Beck ❺ via Red Tarn Beck can be enjoyed, knowing that all of the hard work has been done and there are more swimming spots to discover and enjoy. Once past the old Greenside Mine and the hostel, Glenridding Beck contains some wonderful pebble lined pools, which on a sunny day can keep the swimmer amused until home time. However, it is worth leaving some time, either for the Travellers Rest (the pub on Greenside Road on the descent route) or for another swim in Ullswater ❻ from Glenridding. I have guided a number of groups around this route over the years and the prospect of taking yet another swim at the end of a long day is rarely met with any enthusiasm. Nevertheless, with some gentle insistence to take the plunge, no one has ever regretted it. A swim around Wall Holme or beyond is an amazing tonic and provides the perfect end to a grand day out on one of Lakes finest mountains.

**1** From the car park (which includes the information centre and toilets), cross Glenridding Beck via the road bridge and head west up the road that passes the shops and leads to the Gillside campsite. Follow the road that merges into a track running alongside the beck to Rattlebeck Bridge. Turn left and follow the track that trends south-west and soon zig-zags up to a wall. Go through the gate here and stay on the footpath that follows Mires Beck south-west, up past Little Cove until it hits the wall. The path follows the wall west for a few hundred meters before veering off to the north to skirt around the outcrops under Birkhouse Moor to its summit.
**1.9 miles**

**2** From Birkhouse Moor, stay on the path heading south-west on relatively level terrain, pick up the wall heading in the same direction and follow it to its end at the Hole-in-the-Wall. Stay on the path, still heading south-west, as the route begins to gain height towards Low Spying How and on towards High Spying How, where Striding Edge begins. Follow the obvious path or take in a bit of scrambling if this proves too tame and keep going to the end of the arête and follow the steep ground trending north-west up onto the summit plateau.

Keep an eye out for the memorials and visit the rather inadequate summit cairn at the 950 metre high point, as well as the trig point a little further on, taking in the unique view of the Helvellyn range from the top.
**1.9 miles**

**3** From the trig point at the summit, head north, north-west along the top of the crags for about 100 metres. Take care descending onto Swirral Edge and scramble down the rocky blocks and steps to the arête, following it to the col, where the path cuts down towards the outflow of Red Tarn. The sharp gravel beaches near the outflow provide the best entry points. The tarn is cold, deep and exposed – don't take unnecessary risks and get out while you are still smiling.
**0.7 miles**

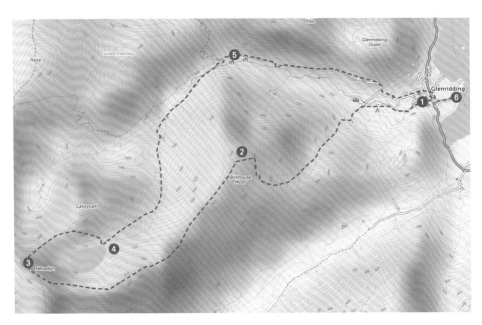

④ Take the descent path that follows the outflow of Red Tarn Beck north-east, following it under the shadow of Catstycam, then north as it begins the steady descent towards Glenridding Common. The path levels out, then zig-zags, before taking a north-easterly course to follow Glenridding Beck. Stay on this route for about 1 kilometre when you can cross the beck by the footbridge at Greenside Mine.
**1.7 miles**

⑤ From the old mine buildings bear east along the rough road, past the YHA and on towards Glenridding. Where you can safely access the beck from the road, do so. A little bit of exploration will reveal some lovely dipping pools.

After a dip or two, continue on the road, ignoring the footpath off to the right after about 1 kilometre and continue onto Greenside Road where the Travellers Rest is to be found. Follow the obvious road back to Glenridding car park, cross the road bridge again and follow the signs to the Ullswater Steamer Pier using the path by the side of the driveway that leads there.

Either side of the Steamer Pier are gently sloping gravel beaches, the perfect place for a little bathing or perhaps some more vigorous swimming out to the islands. Stay well away from the Pier, be aware of the movement of the steamers and hire boats and only swim out to the islands if you are wearing a tow float. It can get very busy here.
**1.9 miles**

⑥ From the pier retrace your steps back to the car park, perhaps stopping for a pub meal on the way.
**0.3 miles**

# Walk 5

# THE TARNS OF PATTERDALE
# AND HARTSOP

This walk takes you to some gems hidden in plain sight, and the chance for a stunningly isolated swim.

In the shadow of High Street, and just off the road between Kirkstone and Patterdale, lie some over-looked wild swimming gems with good parking and a great pub and campsite nearby. It is very easy to drive past Brothers Water and on to Ullswater, but it is worth stopping here purely for the fact that it is one of the quieter parts of the Lakes, despite being among it all, nestled as it is between the more famous peaks and ridges that surround it. I find tarn swimming not unlike Munroe or Corbett collecting – it leads you to magical places that you may not otherwise have discovered.

We begin this walk from the car park at Cow Bridge ❶, but you could use any of the nearby car parks and its location just a few hundred metres from Brothers Water ❷ makes for an easy start to the swimming, which is always a good thing and will put you in a good mood right from the off. For this day out, it pays to make an early start so that you can savour the swimming opportunities without having to rush them to get back in time for last orders!

Formerly known as Broad Water in the 18th century, the story goes that the name was changed to Brothers Water following the tragic accident, which is said to have happened twice, of brothers being drowned there, when one attempted to save the other. On one of the two occasions, the accident happened as they were making an adventurous shortcut to church across the frozen tarn and fell through the ice…so take care churchgoers and ice swimmers alike!

At just about 500 metres wide in every direction and about 16 metres deep, this is one of the smallest lakes in the Lake District and two things always strike me about swimming here: the first is how cool the water is, flowing as it does from a mainly north-

## INFORMATION

DISTANCE: 6.2-7.5 miles
TIME: 8-9 hours
MAP: Harvey British Mountain Map: Lake District, OS Explorer OL5 The English Lakes NE
START/END POINT: Cow Bridge Car Park (NY 403 133, CA11 0NZ)
PUBLIC TRANSPORT: Nearest train station is Penrith. The 508 bus from Penrith stops at the starting point.
SWIMMING: Brothers Water (NY 401 130), Hayeswater (NY 428 126), Angle Tarn (NY 418 143)
PLACES OF INTEREST: Low Hartsop Village, old lead mine workings by Hayeswater Gill and on eastern flank of Hartsop Dodd
REFRESHMENTS: Brothers Water Inn at Kirkstonefoot (017684 82239, CA11 0NZ); White Lion Inn, Patterdale (017684 82214,CA11 0NW); Patterdale Hotel, Patterdale (017684 82231, CA11 0NN)
ACCOMMODATION: Brothers Water Inn and Sykeside Campsite at Kirkstonefoot (01768 482239, CA11 0NZ); The White Lion, Patterdale ( 017684 82214, CA11 0NW); The Patterdale Hotel, Patterdale (017684 82231, CA11 0NN)
WEEKEND SUGGESTION: Stay at the Brothers Water Inn or camp at their Sykeside Campsite and explore either Helvellyn and Red Tarn or the Ullswater fells and swims on your second day.

facing catchment and secondly, how much more lovely the water and view to High Street looks from the western shore than from the road. In the valley tucked under the Hartsop Fells, south of the lake, lies the 16th-century Hartsop Hall, passed to Sir John Lowther in the 17th century; the Lowther Estate still owns vast tracts of land within the region.

The highlight of the swimming here has to be the views and the excellent quality of the water. There are some nice little pebble beaches to swim to and in the warmer months the surface of the water is constantly ringed from the rises of the lively brown trout that live here. This is also the native home of the rare schelly, a bright, silver fish that thrives in clear, well-oxygenated water – a good sign for us swimmers. The lake can get quite weedy in high summer, but not so much that it impedes swimming progress, and the pebbly shoreline with its wooded backdrop and boulder seats is a good place to take breakfast after your swim and perhaps warm up over a pot of tea before contemplating the hike to Hayeswater.

The walk to Hayeswater takes you through the ancient village of Low Hartsop, which lies in the favourite valley of Wainwright who loved it for its old-world charm and lack of obvious tourism so rife in other parts of the Lakes. This lovely village has several 17th-century farm cottages and some still have the spinning rooms where villagers would have made their own clothing, trading surplus produce in the local market towns. Hartsop means 'Valley of the Stag' and I was once lucky enough to startle a very impressive royal stag while descending from High Street and was astonished to see how effortlessly such a large beast could appear to float over the rough fell ground at speed and then evaporate into the distance.

Beyond the small rocky car park at the head of the village road, lies the steep and broad track that takes you up to Hayeswater ❸, which I find a fascinating place to swim as it lies in the moody, hanging trough of Hayeswater Gill. The imposing ridges of High Street and Grey Crag on either side, which begin from the steep V-shaped basin dropping down from Thornthwaite Crag give the place a forlorn atmosphere which accentuates the length of this tarn, which appears more of a mountain mere than a tarn. In his classic book, *The Tarns of Lakeland*, William Heaton Cooper quotes an obscure Alfred Hayes poem about the tarn, and no one expresses the atmosphere there on a stormy mountain day better:

*'Hayeswater'*

*Enfolded in the mountain's naked arms,*
*Where noonday wears a drearier look than night.*

*And echo, like a shrinking anchorite,*
*Wanders unseen, and shadowy strange alarms*
*Visit the soul; there sunshine rarely warms*
*The crags, but only random shafts of light*
*Flit, while the black squalls shrilling from the height*
*Shudder along the lake in scattering swarms.*

*Cradle of tempests, whence the whirlwind leaps*
*To scourge the billows, till they writhe and rear*
*Columns of hissing spray; the wrinkled steeps*
*Scowl at the sullen moaning of the mere;*
*And luminous*
*Against the dale-side drear,*
*Ghostlike, the rainstorm's scanty vesture sweeps.*

Alfred Hayes, *The Vale of Arden:*
*And Other Poems, 1895*

It is the wildness of this place that attracts we outdoorsmen and women, I think. Catch it on a bright and warm summer's day, late morning, when the sun just manages to flood this deep valley beneath the old Roman safe route through Cumbria, and it is a stunning place to be, in foul weather it feels lonely and oppressive.

At just over 900 metres long and 17 metres deep, Hayeswater makes for a good swim and the dramatic, if sometimes dour, scenery just adds to the experience. The dam wall was removed by United Utilities here in 2014 as this was a water supply for Penrith until 2005. The removal of the dam and building of a handy footbridge over the beck have been tastefully done. Although the water depth has dropped by a metre or so, it hasn't affected the swimming much, but it will be nice when the shoreline settles down and drains off a bit. The shoreline is rocky and steep until you reach the head of the valley where it has the feel of a small delta – I once swam the length on the tarn to this spot one moody evening to find a solitary Canada goose sat imperiously on her nest, looking very much at home if a little lonely and out of place.

If you time it right you can be skipping along the path to Angle Tarn ❹ just as the shadows begin to cloak Hayeswater, perhaps enlivened after a good mile or so of mountain swimming and glad to be

on the open fell with far reaching views towards Helvellyn and St Sunday Crag and, in my opinion, the best swim of the day just around the corner.

When I first set eyes on Angle Tarn from the walk that swoops down on it from above, I broke into a trot to get there quicker. It looked so inviting with the low afternoon sun making it shimmer and its mini coves and twin islets giving it a depth of character that you don't often see in our high tarns, due in no small part to the unusual situation of this tarn on a rocky ridge (this being a perfect example of a glacial ridge top, ice scour feature). Angle Tarn lies at 473 metres and is about 350 metres long and 250 metres wide and about 9 metres at its deepest end near Cat Crag and by the outflow of Angle Tarn Beck.

When I last swam here, I disturbed a small gaggle of Canada geese who had made themselves comfortable in the heather on the islets (lacking on the surrounding fell, it being burnt back for sheep grazing) but it was nice to have their company. The tarn was no doubt named after the good angling to be had here, although I've only ever seen the typical tiny dark trout of upland tarns dimpling the water. The swimming is good with just a little weed amongst the water lobelia towards the southernmost shallow end and there are some nice underwater craggy features towards its deepest end by Cat Crag.

A swim here and a last cup of tea from the flask finish the day off nicely and set you up for the steady descent north, north-west back down towards Boredale Hause and perhaps on to Patterdale where good pubs await. If you've no time to visit Patterdale, double back on yourself under Rake Crag when you get to Boredale Hause and take the path south back to Hartsop, where after a short drive to the Brothers Water Inn you can toast a rather grand day out with a glass of ginger beer!

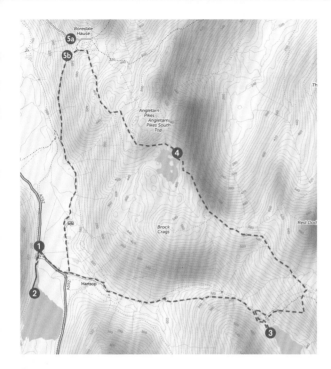

① Park considerately at Cow Bridge near Hartsop and take the obvious riverside path south and upstream towards Brothers Water and after 400 metres or so take the path down to the rocky shore of this lovely little lake.
**0.2 miles**

② Head back the way you came to the car park. From Cow Bridge walk south-east along the road to Hartsop, following the winding little road through the village to the lumpy car park at its head. Go through the gate here and follow the distinct track past the old mine workings and on up towards the steep valley that will come into view to the left. Cross Hayeswater Gill and follow the steep track all the way to Hayeswater. You can get in anywhere but the gravelly beaches to the south of the outflow allow you to avoid most of the sharp rocks and silt exposed along most of the shoreline.
**2.2 miles**

③ From the outflow of Hayeswater, backtrack for about 300 metres and go over the footbridge to take the bridleway that cuts across the fell up towards The Knott, first zigging, then zagging before it meets the right of way that leads to the summit. Turn away from The Knott and head north-west on the footpath, contouring Rest Dodd and on to the ridge that leads you after about 1.2 miles to Angle Tarn.
**1.9 miles**

④ Continue on the path which now snakes off the ridgeline to avoid Angletarn Pikes and Stony Rigg and descends towards the mountain crossroads that is Boredale Hause after another 1.2 miles of walking. There is a confusion of tracks here but dig your compass out and just check your direction before you head off in one of two directions: a) continue north-west to Patterdale, or b) take the bridleway south that leads straight back to Hartsop and Cow Bridge.
**1.2 miles**

⑤ⓐ Continue north-west towards Patterdale approaching via the hamlet of Rooking which leads on to a small road that leads on over the beck and into Patterdale and slake your thirst at the White Lion. Head back the way you came to Rooking but stay on the footpath that runs south along the valley bottom that eventually joins the bridleway coming down the fell from Boredale Hause. Continue on to Hartsop and Cow Bridge.
**1.9 miles**

⑤ⓑ From Boredale Hause take the bridleway south that leads straight back down the fell towards the valley bottom and on towards Hartsop and Cow Bridge.
**0.6 miles**

# BLEA WATER AND SMALL WATER

The backdoor to the Lakes provides classic Lake District walking with exceptional corrie tarn swimming.

*B*lea Water ❷ and Small Water ❸, are two of the finest tarns in Lakeland Mr Alfred Wainright assures us, and who are we to argue? Getting to Mardale Head is an adventure in itself, but once there, the route to these tarns is relatively easy and they are both spectacular, but for different reasons. Mardale Waters is the collective description for the tarns and becks that flow from them and between them they define the character and beauty of the upper Mardale valley.

The hike up from Mardale Head to Blea Water ❶ is rendered more entertaining by the companionship of Mardale Beck and Blea Water Beck. The rush of the water and the sight of so many cascades distracts from the rigours of the climb and provides a foil for the dark, ever-looming view of the mountain cirque above. The view of the tarn enclosed in the steep sides of the glacial bowl, with the fissured crags above is about as dramatic a view as you will find in the Lakes. The tarn lives up to its name of 'dark' or 'dark blue' from the old Norse *blar* and can look 'cold' even on a warm, bright day. Despite that, once in the water and peering into the water with goggles it is full of light and blue-green colour, shafts of sunlight (if present) are rendered distinct and almost physical against the deeper blue of the abyss beneath.

The Brathay Exploration Group, who surveyed all of the tarns of the central Lake District in the 1840s described it thus: "Morphologically this is the finest example of a cirque tarn in England". According to William Heaton Cooper in his *The Tarns of Lakeland*, they had to send for more rope twice before the deepest parts were sounded. Its depth mystified them, but it was proposed that the tarn was so deep due to its location and the action of wind and weather, combined with prolonged glacial erosion and extreme

## INFORMATION

**DISTANCE:** 3 miles, with options to extend the route onto High Street and Mardale III Bell
**TIME:** 2-3 hours walking, 2-3 hours of swimming.
**MAP:** Harvey British Mountain Map: Lake District, OS Explorer OL5 The English Lakes NE
**START/END POINT:** Mardale Head Car Park at the most westerly point of Haweswater (NY 469 107, CA10 2RP)
**SWIMMING:** Blea Water (NY 451 109), Small Water (NY 456 101)
**PLACES OF INTEREST:** Haweswater Reservoir (when water levels are low, the walls and ruins of Mardale Green village can be seen), Haweswater Hotel.
**REFRESHMENTS:** Haweswater Hotel, Bampton, has lots of artefacts on display relating to the lost villages of Mardale and it is a very welcoming place to visit and have a meal or a drink (01931 713673, CA10 2RP).
**ACCOMMODATION:** Haweswater Hotel, Bampton (01931 713673, CA10 2RP). There are many holiday cottages in the villages approaching the reservoir, but no campsites nearby.
**WEEKEND SUGGESTION:** Stay at the Haweswater Hotel for a long weekend and make the most of the opportunities to extend this walk up onto Mardale III Bell, High Street and beyond. While you are at it, explore the shores of Haweswater and Riggindale Beck. There is some good trout fishing from the shore which can fill an afternoon nicely.

moraine deposits. Whatever actually happened back in the Ice Age, it produced a damn fine swimming pool for us today.

The Brathay survey, complicated by the strong downdraft from the winds coming over High Street affecting the stability of their little boat, revealed it to be one of the deepest bodies of water in the district at 63 metres in depth. Only Windermere and Wastwater are deeper. To dive down as deep as you dare in its clear oligotrophic waters is an experience not to be forgotten; its depths seem endless, and as a situation for mountain swimming it is awe inspiring.

The hill walking here is wonderful too and quite literally takes you on a walk through history. This route can be extended from Blea Water, heading north up to Riggindale Crag ridge, onto High Street to Racecourse Hill, Mardale Ill Bell and down the Nan Bield Pass to Small Water… although this course of action can eat into valuable swimming time. If you are more of a hill walker, perhaps take the high route as well as a picnic, up onto the flat summit of Racecourse Hill above Blea Water and imagine the spectacle of the farmers meets and summer fairs held there up until the 19th century. It must have been quite a sight to witness the horse racing and local sports of the day in such a setting and they must have been a fit bunch to even contemplate such a thing.

The walk to Small Water ❷ follows an unlikely trod across the steep ground right under Piot Crag, crossing both the north and east spurs of the crag and is immensely satisfying. To find a route between two high tarns that does not require a serious expenditure of energy is rare, and this route quickly leads to the short descent off the east spur to the tarn. Where Blea Water is dark and dramatic, Small Water has an open and light aspect for a corrie tarn and is blessed with shingle beaches bordered by lush grass and rush, a small satellite tarn to the east and the ancient thoroughfare of Nan Bield Pass hugging its shoreline. It is nothing short of beautiful and it is sure to bring a smile to the swim hiker's face on cresting the ridge. It contains brown trout and some rare Ullswater schelly which were introduced in the 1980s and on a calm day you can watch the trout rising to the fly before plunging in to join them.

The stoutly built stone shelters on the shores of Small Water give an insight into to the importance of the route that leads steeply up to Nan Bield Pass. The pass leads on to the ridges that connected many historically important places, and these shelters would have provided protection in a storm or during unplanned benightment. The shelters are distinctly coffin like, but are cosy enough for one, once wriggled inside and they provide good protection during severe wind and weather. Your author has used them on more than one occasion to warm up and get a brew on, after cold late season swims in the tarn.

Naturally, Small Water is a grand place for a swim, and one could quite happily spend the day here, swimming, picnicking and exploring the ridge routes to the summit of Mardale Ill Bell.

From medieval times, and possibly even earlier, there was significant demand for the rocks and

minerals to be found in the Cumbrian mines. Hill passes were important not only for the local sheep farmers, but for the safe movement of goods (and soldiers during Roman times). The Romans relied on the high passes and broad ridge routes for travel between their forts, the old Roman road is still visible on High Street which towers above the Mardale Waters. At the time the long steep sided valleys were densely forested, leaving them and any other traveller prone to ambuscade.

Centuries of charcoal burning for mineral extraction followed by the demands of the Industrial revolution have cleared the forests, and since the Eighteenth century the mountains and their passes were looked upon by the Lakes Poets as places of beauty rather than fear and promoted as such. A sentiment that we mountain swimmers are lucky enough to share to this day along with the freedom to travel the passes for recreation rather than for survival. The descent route follows the pass down the course of Small Water Beck and is as enjoyable as the ascent. It delivers the walker efficiently down to the valley floor and Mardale Head and the enjoyable trip back alongside the shores of Haweswater, one of our loveliest reservoirs.

The lovely waters of Haweswater Reservoir hide the walls and ruins of Mardale Green Village, which can be spotted when water levels are low. The village was flooded in 1935 when the Manchester Corporation dammed the existing Haweswater, raising the water level to form the reservoir. The Rigg can be reached from Mardale Head and when the water is really low one can walk to the island of Wood Howe. Take yourself to the Haweswater Hotel (built to replace the Dunn Bull Inn which was flooded when the dam was completed) after your walk for some refreshment and to take in the displays of artefacts of the lost villages of Mardale.

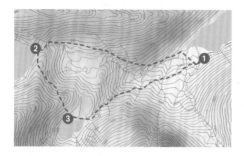

**1** From the car park, go through the obvious, outsized deer gate to the south-west which leads to Gatesgarth Pass. After a few meters turn right, following the signpost for Riggindale and the fence, heading north-west, cross the two bridges over Mardale Beck and turn left following the footpath west. The path ascends gradually, following the course of the beck, until another deer gate is passed and the path trends away from the beck and up steeper ground trending north west.

The path levels off at the shallow coomb before the final push alongside the cascade of Blea Water Beck when the first tantalising glimpse of the corrie comes into view, closely followed by the welcome sight of Blea Water. The best access to the water is right by the small dam as the banks of the tarn are all rather steep elsewhere.
**1.2 miles**

**2** From just below the dam at Blea Water, cross Blea Water Beck, and head steeply up onto

the north spur of Piot Crag. After the steep initial climb onto the spur, it levels out and a small but distinct trod heads south, south east, contouring perfectly under Piot Crag and its outlying crags above. The trod leads out onto steep ground and past some small stone ruins, but is a good path with airy views into the coomb beneath, and soon leads up to the broad eastern spur of Piot Crag.

Small Water and its satellite tarnlet is visible from the crest of the spur. Head steeply down into the corrie, following the trod that snakes down to the north shore of the tarn. There

are nice pebble beaches dotted about the shoreline and a good path circles most of the tarn and even the steeper western shore is accessible.
**0.6 miles**

**3** To descend back to the car park, take the good path on the east side of Small Water Beck, the outflow of the tarn. The descent is very enjoyable and follows the tumbling waters of the beck until it reaches a deer gate. From here the path aims for the valley bottom below and finally levels out at the gate in the wall which is only a few hundred meters from the car park.
**1.2 miles**

# Walk 7

# THE FALLS OF SWINDALE

A rewarding walk to the little known vale of
Swindale and quite possibly, some of the best
waterfall pools in the Lakes. Well worth the
long drive to get there.

## INFORMATION

DISTANCE: 7.2 miles
TIME: 5 hours
MAP: Harvey British Mountain Map:
Lake District, OS Explorer OL5 The
English Lakes NE
START/END POINT: Filter House
Roadside (NY 521 144, nearest
postcode CA10 2QT).
PUBLIC TRANSPORT: The nearest
train station is Penrith but unfortunately
no public transport to Swindale. On
Thursdays the Fellranger 111 bus from
Penrith Bus Station stops at Bampton
Grange. The best way to get there is
by bicycle, car, hire car or taxi.
SWIMMING: Forces Falls (NY 509 113)
PLACES OF INTEREST: Haweswater
Reservoir, Sleddale Hall - Uncle
Monty's cottage 'Crow Crag' of cult
film Withnail and I fame (now a private
residence), Wet Sleddale Reservoir
(for fly fishing – or try it Withnail
style!), Aira Force Waterfall, Lowther
Castle and gardens, the Simon Stone
(NY 504 116).
REFRESHMENTS: Withnail fans can
drink the finest wines available at The
Crown and Mitre Inn in Bampton
Grange (01931 713225, CA10 2QR).
Granny Dowbekins Tea Rooms, Pooley
Bridge, a bit of a drive away but great
(017684 86453, CA10 2NP). Shap
Chippy, Shap, no frills, but good quick
food if returning this way (01931
716060, CA10 3JS). Bampton Village
Café & Shop, Brampton (01931
713351, CA10 2RQ).
NEARBY SWIM SPOTS: The Mardale
Waters, Blea Water and Small Water,
the Tarns of Patterdale and Hartsop.

W ainwright wrote about Swindale in both his *The Far Eastern Fells* and *The Outlying Fells of Lakeland* guides. He implores us no to tell too many folk about it as the valley is so unspoilt and I am not ashamed to urge you to do the same!

Swindale is a handsome valley and enjoys a fraction of the footfall of the more popular Lakeland valleys, although as Lake District fells go Swindale Common and its neighbour Mardale Common are rather plain and don't offer particularly good views. Nevertheless, the gnarly east face of Selside Pike as seen from Swindale is a marvellous sight and makes up for its bleak neighbours amply. Split by the jagged cleft of Hobgrumble Gill and wreathed in black crags it draws the eye away from the plain grassy summits surrounding it and invites further investigation.

The moraine deposits and large boulders dotted about the beck hint at the glacial action which occurred in the valley. At the base of Hobgrumble Gill lies Dodd Bottom, the location of a dried up tarn bed as well as the Simon Stone, a large boulder left stranded by the side of the beck which lies between a grove of weathered trees at the dogleg before the falls. It can be reached by crossing the beck at the footbridge upstream. It has a number of bouldering problems on it for any budding climbers in your walking group and is a nice place to visit if you are taking the alternative return route suggested in the directions. Without question though, the highlight of this remote dale is the series of falls to the east of this extensive amphitheatre.

Swindale Beck cascades down the gorge at Forces Falls ❷ in a series of ribbon-like falls and pools, before sweeping through

the moraine at its base to continue its more mundane meanderings towards the River Lowther. Wainwright held Forces Falls in the same esteem as Aira Force and, were he a swimming man, may also have compared them to the likes of Black Moss Pot or Buckstones Jump. To get to either of these swimming locations involves expending a considerable about of energy to swim in very small places… for a very good reason: they are the Special Places. The pools of Forces Falls give the gift of intimate swimming in a fairy tale setting to the swimmer, with clear amber water and plunging falls at their head. If the upper Esk was a bit too crowded for you, then this is where you'll feel at home.

At the top of the Forces Falls the beck keeps on giving, as the ground begins to level out there is one final limpid pool to explore before the return journey. One could be forgiven for turning around at this point and doing it all again, begging the question: can you have too much of a good thing? But turn around we must, or at least press on. An alternative to the route given here is to seek out the path that ascends from the valley floor and retrace one's steps back to Dodd Bottom and beyond. But to visit Selside Pike ❸ and the glimpse what flows from Hobgrumble Gill press on.

Anyone with an aversion to navigation will be delighted by the ascent to Selside Pike from the falls. A handy fence crosses the path at Swine Gill and leads all the way to the summit. As it does so it leads across the hanging valley above Hobgrumble Gill, and there is value in taking a small detour to peer down the gill to the falls beneath, which are spectacular. The grassy expanse of Selside is broken momentarily at the summit, which is a jumble of rocks forming a cairn-shelter combination. Wainwright surmises that a rocky outcrop was broken up to form the cairn here which seems very probable. From the summit there are good views across to Shap and the Pennines, otherwise the view is fairly plain but the romp down to the Old Corpse Road is pleasant enough.

The track of the Corpse Road was used by the parishioners of Mardale to take their dead to the consecrated ground in Shap. It must have been a grim journey for those in mourning but provides a very effective means of descent into Swindale. Back on the road the return journey passes quickly, hopefully leaving time to visit The Crown and Mitre for a drink, just go easy on the Withnail quotes… the poor things have heard it all a thousand times before!

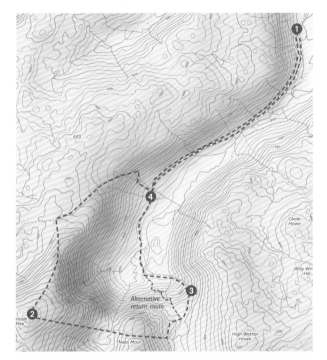

south-west until the terrain levels out. From the beck, head due west to pick up the main bridleway path coming up from the valley bottom.

From here an alternative descent can be made straight back down to Dodd Bottom to return via the approach route.

Carry on south along the bridleway for a few hundred metres to Swine Gill and the fence that cuts right across the path. Turn right to follow the fence line west and climb to the broad spur of Nabs Moor. Cross the hanging valley at the head of Hobgrumble Gill (go and steal a look at the falls) and ascend to Selside Pike, an easy prospect, just follow the fence.
**1.2 miles**

❸ From Selside Pike head north, north-east down the spur following any of the small paths towards Selside End. Just over a kilometre from the summit the Old Corpse Road is reached at a wooden marker post. Turn right here following the track east, north-east and keep going as the track descends beneath Thorny Knott, zig-zags down and heads straight into Swindale Head.
**1.7 miles**

❹ From Swindale Head, head back along Swindale Lane to return to the roadside parking near the Filter House.
**1.5 miles**

❶ Park thoughtfully by the roadside just south-west of Filter House. Continue walking along Swindale Lane, and keep going past Swindale Foot Farm for a further kilometre where the track runs close to Swindale Beck at the footbridge at Truss Gap House. Carry on the road for another 1.2 kilometres to reach the farm at Swindale Head.

From Swindale Head follow the bridleway heading roughly south through the meadows and gates and cross the plank footbridge over the gill at Dodd Bottom. The path threads through a series of moraines and 250 metres on from the footbridge the bridleway passes very close to the beck. Here leave the path and follow the beck heading off at just south of east. As the river bends around to the south the terrain steepens, and the beck gets more interesting. There are lovely pools all of the way up, but the best of the Forces Falls, with deep and inviting pools, are to be found just before the beck levels out.
**2.8 miles**

❷ From Forces Falls carry on following the beck south,

*Walk 8*

# CATBELLS AND THE DERWENTWATER SHORELINE

Classic hillwalking, unbeatable scenery and endless swimming opportunities along the Derwentwater shoreline make this a walk you will want to return to again and again.

*D*erwentwater vies with Windermere as the most popular lake in the district. Although I have the good fortune to call Windermere 'home' so to speak, the grander scenery, larger islands, and excellent lakeshore access win me over every time I swim here. For the visiting swim hiker, the proximity of Keswick also has a certain draw. Keswick has been a destination for pilgrims visiting Saint Herbert's Island since the 14th century and more recently since the advent of tourism in the region from the late 18th century. It offers a strategic base from which to launch every kind of outdoor foray and is full of good accommodation of every kind as well as a vibrant pub and café culture, powered by the walkers, climbers, cyclists, paddlers, sailors and swimmers who are drawn to the North Lakes.

Derwentwater is very accessible from Keswick and a short walk through the town, past Crow Park and the Theatre by the Lake, will take you to its shore. Indeed, the motivated visitor could keep going at this point, on past Friar's Crag and Strandshag Bay to walk around the entire lake, which is a wonderful day out (but leaves little time for swimming). The history of the lake is varied and interesting and is full of literary associations thanks to the artists and writers who have been drawn to the area since the 18th century. However, the real appeal of Derwentwater to the swimmer, aside from its ease of access, is its islands and impressive mountain scenery. The finest views are to the south and west towards High Spy and Catbells, Causey Pike and Hopegill Head (the Derwent Fells), and further south still to the impressive skyline of Borrowdale. They give a thrilling sense of place to a swimmer at lake level and being surrounded by these great chunks of rock make any swim here more meaningful.

## INFORMATION

**DISTANCE:** 5 miles
**TIME:** 4 hours
**MAP:** Harvey British Mountain Map: Lake District, OS Explorer OL4 The English Lakes NW
**START/END POINT:** Roadside parking near to (but not at) Hawse End Outdoor Centre, Portinscale (NY 246 211, nearest postcode CA12 5UE)
**PUBLIC TRANSPORT:** Honister Rambler Service 77/77A runs between Keswick and Catbells during the summer season. Regular buses link Keswick to Penrith, Windermere and Workington stations and occasionally Carlisle. The Keswick Launch Company operates a regular shuttle service between Keswick and Hawse End between April and October. A less regular service calls at Hawse End during November and March.
**SWIMMING:** Great Bay (NY 256 189), Myrtle Bay (NY 255 191), Otterbield Bay (NY 251 209)
**PLACES OF INTEREST:** Whinlatter Forest Park, Keswick Launch Company, Theatre by the Lake, Threlkeld Quarry and Mining Museum, Watendlath Trout Fishery, Honister Slate Mine
**REFRESHMENTS:** Nichol End Cafe at Nichol End Marine, Portinscale (017687 73082, CA12 5TY); The Chalet Tearooms & Restaurant, Portinscale (017687 72757, CA12 5RF); The Lingholm Kitchen, The Lingholm Estate, Portinscale (017687 71206, CA12 5TZ)
**EASIER ACCESS:** Good access to Derwentwater at Crow Park in Keswick and Strandshag Bay.

Like all large lakes surrounded by mountains, the mood of both water and scenery is constantly changing with the weather and all of the expected extremes can be encountered within a single swim. This is particularly true when venturing away from the shoreline to explore the islands. Thrilling though it may be, extreme care must be taken in this case, as the visibility of the ever circulating motor launches can be seriously reduced even with a small amount of chop, leaving the unwitting swimmer dangerously vulnerable to collision. It is good form to always wear a tow float on any large and busy lake and Derwentwater is no exception. Be as visible and alert as you can so that everyone can enjoy your adventure.

There are four large islands on Derwentwater: Lord's Island, Derwent Island, St Herbert's Island and Rampsholme Island. The smaller islands, dotted about the perimeter are Park Neb, Otter Island and Otterbield Island. Swimming to an island has a unique appeal that only swimmers will relate to, and all of the Derwentwater Islands are worth a visit. If you have the time, some of the best of them can be taken in during this walk and are discussed later on in this chapter.

Of course, the swimming is great, we're in the Lakes after all, but let's not forget the walking. From Keswick, every point of the compass leads towards classic hill walking too. The walk up Catbells ❷ has been the introduction to Lake District walking for many a young pioneer and although very well-trodden is a real gem. I distinctly remember my first ascent of Catbells as a child; it filled me with wonder and awe for the surrounding fells that remains with me to this day. You will meet every kind of walker on Catbells, and it is always a pleasure to see such a broad mix of generations deriving so much enjoyment from being outdoors.

The walk to the summit begins in woodland and rises out onto the soaring fells that eventually lead on to the greater heights of Maiden Moor, High Spy and Dale Head. Every foot of ascent gives better and better views of the lake and into the Borrowdale Valley to the south. The ascent is never too taxing, and every step is a joy as time passes quickly with such beautiful panoramas to enjoy along the way. Even the descent is pleasant with the steepest section being the short drop down to Hause Gate before the path cuts gently across the contour lines to the broad valley below.

Here the route picks up the Cumbria Way which crosses the flood plains surrounding Ellers Beck and leads to Derwentwater where the swimming begins. As previously mentioned, there is good swimming everywhere on Derwentwater but for the sake of optimising swimming quality it is best to focus on two areas, the first being the bays and small islands of the south-west shore. Great Bay ❸ which contains Park Neb, Myrtle Bay and Abbot's Bay which contains Otter Island and Brandelhow Bay both offer exquisite swimming along the prettiest section of the lake. The second area is the Otterbield Bay ❹ further north along the shore towards the beginning of the walk. This bay presents the opportunity to link the tiny Otterbield Island and St Herbert's Island. It is a notable swim of about 2,000 metres to the largest of Derwentwater's islands which has a fascinating history of interesting visitors including both saints and squirrels.

St Herbert of Derwentwater was a close friend and disciple of St Cuthbert of Lindisfarne. It was at Cuthbert's request that he became an anchorite (one who lives in religious isolation), living for many years on the island that now bears his name. He ate fish from the lake and grew vegetables on the land around his cell leading a simple life of prayer and meditation. Pilgrims visited him on occasion and continued to visit his cell on the island well after his death. Friars' Crag is named after the monks who came in pilgrimage to visit the saint by boat. The indistinct remains of his cell can still be made out in the undergrowth today if you are determined to find them. Herbert and Cuthbert died on the same day, 20 March 687 and share the same feast day.

St Herbert's Island inspired Beatrix Potter in her creation of Owl Island in *The Tale of Squirrel Nutkin*. In the story Nutkin, his brother Twinkleberry and the rest of the red squirrel family sailed over to the island to collect nuts on tiny rafts, using their tails as sails. Disappointingly, I've never seen a squirrel or an owl on the island, but it is justifiably popular with the adventurous souls that live in or frequent the North Lakes. The island never seems crowded, but it is often occupied by bushcrafters who have paddled out to spend the night under the stars, or boaters (and the occasional swimmer) who just want to stop there and rest in such a peaceful place, admiring the view for a while.

Once swimming adventures have been concluded at Otterbield Bay, it is not so far to get back to the car, or to meet the boat at Hawse End landing. Then perhaps it is time to end the day at one of Portinscale's fine cafés or with fish and chips in Keswick marketplace outside the Moot Hall.

Alternative island swims can be made from other locations around Derwentwater. Derwent Isle is best reached from Crow Park, or from Friar's Crag (avoid the busy landing stage area). This large island is owned by the National Trust and is rented out to private tenants. It is dominated by a very grand-looking house with a lush lawn running down to its south-facing shore. Landing is not allowed but the house is open to the public five days throughout the year. It makes for a nice swim within easy walking distance from Keswick.

Calf Close Bay on the eastern shore offers a satisfying island-hopping swimming loop by linking together Rampsholme Island, St Herbert's Island and Lord's Island. The swimming between each island never exceeds 700 metres and it is nice to have a little break on the gravel spits of each island before returning to the bay.

The major islands and much of the shoreline is owned by the National Trust. There are many nesting geese and ducks in the spring on all of the islands on Derwentwater. Take care not to disturb the wildlife at this time of year, in particular on Lord's Island. The situation regarding New Zealand Pygmy Weed should also be mentioned here. This non-native invasive species is everywhere in Derwentwater and forms dense mats on the lake bed. The National Trust do a great job of keeping it in check – please do your bit by checking your gear, wetsuit, or swimming costume for bits of weed. Even tiny bits can spread this damaging weed to other bodies of water. Check, clean and thoroughly dry anything used in this lake before swimming elsewhere.

As previously mentioned in the introduction to this chapter, a complete circumnavigation of the lake can be made directly from Keswick. Follow the Cumbria Way out of town and all the way around the western side of the lake. The River Derwent can be crossed at the Chinese Bridge then by following the road and paths that run alongside the eastern shore, a return to Keswick can be made. For the fit adventure swimmer this offers many opportunities for exploration by combining swimming with walking and/or running.

**1** Take the small path east from the roadside parking near Hawse End for about 200 metres. Turn south onto the well-worn zig-zagging footpath and follow this on to the spur of Skelgill Bank which heads south-west. Stay on the easy-to-follow path, past the memorial tablet to Thomas Arthur Leonard and all the way to the high point of Skelgill Bank at 338 metres. Here the path drops down, passing the old Brandley Mine workings before the final ascent to Catbells.

Continue steadily uphill on the same path which undulates as it steepens into an easy rocky stairway which leads up to the summit tower of Catbells.

**1 mile**

**2** From Catbells remain on the well-trodden path which bears south, past Mart Bield and down to the broad col below. At the broad plateau of the col lies a crossroads, take the left-hand path heading east and follow it down to Hause Gate and the steep zig-zags below it. Here the path follows the easiest line of descent across the fell in a south-easterly direction until it joins the old green road next to the wooded edge of Manesty Park. Stay on the track until it joins the Grange Road below at Manesty. Turn right at the road and follow it for 250 metres then turn left onto the Cumbria Way path that follows Ellers Beck to the north-east.

Follow the winding Cumbria Way to the mixed woodland and carry on through the gate. Once out of the woods take the path to the left at the fork crossing the field, still on a north-easterly course until you can see the lake. At the T-junction in the path turn left, then almost immediately right, coming off the Cumbria Way path to head directly to the lakeshore. This is Great Bay, an ideal place to launch an investigative swim to the little Park Neb Island and to continue on around to the other intimate bays to the north. This can of course be done as one big swim, or a series of dips, as there is a footpath that leads all the way around to Myrtle Bay before re-joining the Cumbria Way which leads on to the other bays mentioned in the introduction.

**1.9 miles**

**3** Leave Great Bay where you came in to re-join the Cumbria Way path (or follow it round to Myrtle Bay as suggested above) and stay on this delightful lakeshore path all the way to Otterbield Bay, a distance of about 1¼ miles. Keswick Launch Company have landing stages just above Brandelhow Bay and Victoria Bay which can be used to provide an alternative route back to Keswick by boat if you so choose.

At Otterbield Bay the adventurous swimmer can head off for a tour of Otterbield and St Herbert's Islands (bearing in mind that this route crosses the path of the motor launches) or be content with swimming within the bay itself, which is a very pleasant, relatively risk-free option.

**1.7 miles**

**4** From Otterbield Bay regain the path heading north and which soon heads north-west through the woods until it joins another track which soon passes Hawse End Outdoor Centre.

Just past the centre, broad footpaths head east and then west. Take the easterly path to return to the lakeshore to get the launch at the landing stage there. Take the westerly path to get back to the cattle grid and the roadside car park.

**0.4 miles**

*Walk 9*

# HARROP AND BLEA TARN

Wild swimming in Harrop Tarn and the less visited Blea Tarn and a return via High Tove and the delightful, wooded shores of Thirlmere.

## INFORMATION

DISTANCE: 7.5 miles
TIME: 6 hours
MAP: Harvey British Mountain Map: Lake District, OS Explorer OL4 The English Lakes NW & OS Explorer OL5 The English Lakes NE
START/END POINT: Dob Gill Car Park (NY 315 140, CA12 4TP)
PUBLIC TRANSPORT: Nearest train station is Windermere. The A591 road is served by the 555 bus route between Windermere and Keswick. Walk from the stop at Wythburn.
SWIMMING: Harrop Tarn (NY 310 136), Blea Tarn (NY 292 141)
PLACES OF INTEREST: The Tottling Stone at Launchy Gill, Castlerigg Stone Circle
REFRESHMENTS: The Kings Head Inn, Thirlspot (017687 72393, CA12 4TN). Great cafés and pubs in Keswick to the north and Grasmere to the south.
NEARBY SWIM SPOTS: Dock Tarn, Watendlath Tarn (ask permission from the fishery office prior to swimming), Grisedale Tarn, Grasmere, Rydal Water, Bassenthwaite lakes

W ainwright is scathing about the central fells of this region. He describes the Wythburn Valley as a study in desolation and suggests that Armboth Fell is not worth the effort! He is full of praise however for the views from Fisher Crag and the forested and craggy fell side that overlooks Thirlmere. Even local man William Gilpin savaged the area in his 1772 Observations of Cumberland and Westmoreland. He thought the old lake of Thirlmere (before it was flooded) and the surrounding fells as savage and desolate. Although we can forgive him this, being as he was an aesthete and originator of the idea of the picturesque. He was no doubt particularly fussy about his countryside vistas.

*"It can be said of very few fells that they are not really worth climbing; Armboth Fell is one of the few."* Arthur Wainwright.

As a swimmer as well as a mountaineer, I feel that I must stick up for the Wythburn Fells. Boggy they may be, but they are home to some damn good swimming and the mixed woodland that now flourishes along the borders of Thirlmere is a pleasure to walk through. I make no apology then for this route that aims to make the best of both and leave it to the reader to make their own conclusions about its worth; just remember to pack a spare pair of socks.

The steep walk up through the pine trees is enhanced by the views of Helvellyn to the east and by the attractive falls and cascades of Dob Gill. It is a shame that the plantation is so dense alongside the gill, as there are some wonderful pools there that really catch the morning sun. The adventurous swimmer, armed with machete, pruning saw and rope could entertain themselves all day exploring the dipping opportunities to be had in the gill, although it would be dangerous work. The trees here were planted without much thought, although they do reduce runoff into the reservoir. Thankfully there are plans afoot to return the Thirlmere forests back to a more natural woodland, no doubt increasing biodiversity along with its visual appeal.

Emerging from the dense woodland into the open space surrounding Harrop Tarn ❷ is always a pleasant surprise. The hike to the top passes quicker than expected, although this may be due to the anticipation of the swim. First impressions, drawn from the immediate surroundings and encroaching mass of sedge, water horsetail and yellow water lily is that there is not much water here to swim in at all. But never fear, access to the water is via the only gravel beach bordering the tarn at the small inflow of Mosshause Gill on the northern shoreline and there is enough to entertain outdoor swimmers. The tarn is often colder than expected and has a wonderful golden colour if the sunlight is streaming through it as you swim, encouraging the odd dive to the roots of the lilies to gaze up through the shimmering water.

The tarn lies in a hollow in a small plateau, and Tarn Crags forms a backwall some 300 metres to the south-west of the tarn, but it would be inaccurate to describe it as a corrie tarn, although it is held in place by a large amount of glacial debris. The rocky outflow shows some fine *roches moutonnées*, an indicator of the glacial scouring which shaped the features underlying what we see today. Ullscarf Gill has infilled the area with deposits and one is always left with the impression that the tarn will no longer be there in the years ahead, so make the most of your time here! The bog surrounding the tarn is a 'schwingmoor', or 'quaking bog' formed by sphagnum mosses growing across the surface and is typical of small

acidic tarns like this. At Harrop it covers over half of the tarn surface area, the original tarn area is defined by the edges of the plantation which now stand some distance from the present shoreline.

The hike up towards Blea Tarn ❸ follows the meander of Mosshause Gill which flows into Harrop Tarn, and threads through a lush mixed woodland dotted with great outcrops of sphagnum moss. The path carries on up to the headwaters of the gill and onto the 'desolation' of Armboth Fell before cresting its broad ridge and descending to the Blea Tarn.

Blea Tarn at Armboth has a nice open aspect. It lies on an open gently sloping valley on the ridge top between Watendlath and Armboth Fells. It lacks any significant backwall, although there are various rocky outcrops emanating from Coldbarrow Fell around its south-west shore. It has a rocky bottom most of the way in from the shoreline and holds lots of minnows and some good sized trout, which is a sure sign of healthy water if ever there was one. On a nice, still day the swimming here is sublime, but it can feel bleak and exposed in poor or windy weather. The last time we visited with friends it was autumn and freezing cold, but we all had a very enjoyable dip and warmed up in the late season sun during a picnic in the rush.

From Blea Tarn, fit and enthusiastic tarn enthusiasts could also seek out Dock Tarn (NY 274 144) or Launchy Gill Tarn (NY 301 150) as detailed in Don Blair's excellent book *Exploring Lakeland Tarns*. This adds some considerable mileage to the route and requires good navigational skills but these interesting tarns, both very different in character, are certainly worth the effort if the weather is fine.

The much besmirched broad boggy ridge of Armboth Fell leads past Shivery Man and Middle Crag before reaching High Tove and the descent

to Fisher Gill and Armboth ④ itself. Here commences the walk along Thirlmere, where swimming is strictly forbidden, on pain of death. Mercifully the lovely shoreline can be enjoyed whether swimming or not, and if the water level in the reservoir is not too low, the banks look very natural, and the walk through the mixed woodland is very enjoyable. The islands visible off the shoreline are Deergarth How Island, which is a bird sanctuary, and Hawes How Island. Both are vigorously protected by the current custodians of the water, United Utilities, who allow no access to the islands. This is somewhat understandable, but still a shame, although access to the water by canoe and sailing boat is allowed (put in at Armboth).

Thirlmere is well established as part of the Lake District scenery now but caused something of a stir when the idea was first proposed. The concept of the reservoir was particularly denounced by John Ruskin who branded the Manchester Corporation (who were in charge of developments) as thieves and robbers. Despite the furore, four years of construction work saw both the reservoir and aqueduct open in 1894. Thirlmere is the longest gravity-fed aqueduct in Britain with no pumps required anywhere along the route. It remains an engineering marvel and the virtually unseen 96 mile Thirlmere Aqueduct still supplies Manchester and Keswick with water to this day.

Dobgill and the car park are eventually reached after the walk along the Thirlmere path where feet can be dried out and plans made for refreshment. The best place to warm up, dry out and to get a good meal is the Kings Head just up the road on the A591, although the excellent pubs and restaurants of both Keswick and Grasmere are not far away and offer enough variety for every taste.

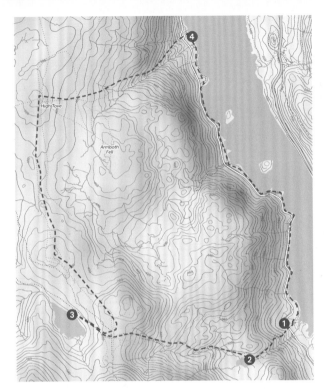

bearing until the edge of the forest is reached about 500 metres from the track junction.

From here the path follows one of the tributaries of Mosshause Gill up the side of the open fell. The going is tough on steep and boggy ground but after another 500 metres it levels out to meet the fence which divides the broad coll all the way to High Tove and beyond.

Go over the stile and stay on the path, heading down to the north-eastern shore of Blea Tarn which will be visible below. The north-east shore offers the most convenient place from which to swim and explore the rest of the tarn.
**1.4 miles**

**3** Regain the path and head back to the stile over the fence at the col. Go over the stile, turn left, and follow the boggy path that runs alongside the fence heading roughly north-west. Pass the tarnlet, cross the fence ahead, which leads away from the broad ridge towards Launchy Gill, and continue on the path following the ridge fence to gain height at Shivery Knott and Middle Crag about 1 kilometre from the last fence junction.

Continue following the fence for another 600 metres, heading almost due north to reach the cairn at High Tove and the crossed paths. Take the path to the right heading east and savour the final

**1** From Dob Gill Car Park take the obvious footpath heading south-west which heads straight up the forested fellside, following the course of Dob Gill. The hard climbing soon relents as the path levels and the abrupt exit from the dense forest reveals Harrop Tarn.

By all means explore the outflow into Dob Gill and its stepping stones but continue around the tarn to the right to visit the north shore. From the track follow the rather boggy inflow of Mosshause Gill to the small gravel spit. The

water here is at its deepest and offers the best swimming option.
**0.4 miles**

**2** Return to the main track at Mosshause Gill and follow the woodland track west, north-west for about 200 metres to meet the junction with another track. Cut the corner to follow the left hand track which continues straight on in the west, north-westerly direction. The track here becomes very confused, but never fear, all paths lead in the same direction, just remain on a west, north-west

kilometre of boggy descent down to Fishercrag Plantation. Cross the wall and continue down the path running parallel to Fisher Gill until the road is reached at Armboth on Thirlmere.
**3.2 miles**

④ From Armboth follow the footpath roughly south along the shores of Thirlmere. About 1 kilometre from Armboth a small promontory points the way to Deergarth How Island and a few hundred meters on from here the path crosses Launchy Gill.

The reach below the gill gives good views out to Hawes How Island and leads to the craggy Hause Point. From the Point, the path carries on for another kilometre or so before reaching Dob Gill and the path up to the road and Dob Gill car park.
**2.5 miles**

## Walk 10

# BLACKMOSS POT, GALLENY FORCE AND THE FAIRY GLEN

A journey to Dipping Heaven and one of the most enchanting valleys in the Lakes.

**T**he swimming in this valley will delight all those who revel in spontaneous dipping. If like myself, you struggle to walk past an inviting river pool without stripping off for a swim then this may be a very long walk for you! Whenever I head up the Langstrath my love of playing in the water is instantly rekindled and always adds to this grand day out. In addition to the dipping opportunities there are also the ancient woodlands that cling to the dramatic fellside to explore.

The woods are as delightful as the becks. These are the Atlantic Oakwoods, the temperate rain forests that once cloaked much of the western seaboard of Europe, now home to secretive and often unobserved wildlife. Listen out for buzzards and peregrine falcons soaring overhead. The raven is relatively common throughout the valley and during the summer months the striking pied flycatcher takes up residence in the forest. Roe Deer are often seen in the woodlands and the larger Red Deer can be found on the high fells above the tree line.

On the ground these ancient pastures reveal an incredible diversity of plants, particularly ferns, and a dazzling array of mosses and liverworts. The Borrowdale Valley has a nationally significant collection of outstanding rare lichens and a rich variety of fungi in the autumn. Borrowdale is one of the last bastions of the red squirrel in Cumbria, so keep your eyes peeled. The beer garden of the Langstrath Inn can be a good place to spot them on a quiet afternoon.

You can dip and swim at any time all along this route, but it is good to arrive at Blackmoss Pot ❸ early as there is so much to do and see in this valley that an early start is essential to fit it all in. Known as Blackmoor Pot in years past, it offers those who appreciate solitude a moment to themselves; it is a popular

## INFORMATION

**DISTANCE:** 6.2 miles
**TIME:** 3 hours walking, 1-2 hours swimming and dipping
**MAP:** Harvey British Mountain Map: Lake District, OS Explorer OL4 The English Lakes NW
**START/END POINT:** Rosthwaite National Trust Car Park (NY 257 148, CA12 5XB)
**PUBLIC TRANSPORT:** Nearest train stations are Windermere or Penrith. From Windermere, take the 555 bus to Keswick, from Penrith take the X5 or X4. From Keswick take 77a (April to October) or 78 to Rosthwaite.
**PARKING:** Rosthwaite National Trust Car Park (NY 257 148, CA12 5XB) or Borrowdale Institute. The Scafell Hotel (CA12 5XB) also has a public car park, they charge £3/day. Please don't park in the village of Stonethwaite.
**SWIMMING:** Blackmoss Pot (NY 267 113), Langstrath Pools and Galleny Force Pools (& Fairy Glen), (NY 273 131).
**PLACES OF INTEREST:** The Bowder Stone, Watendlath, Ashness Bridge, Lodore Falls, Castle Crag, Holy Trinity Church at Grange.
**REFRESHMENTS:** The Flock-In Tea Room at Yew Tree Farm, Rosthwaite, (017687 77675, CA12 5XB); The Royal Oak, Rosthwaite (017687 77214, CA12 5XB); Scafell Hotel, Rosthwaite (017687 77208, CA12 5XB); The Langstrath Country Inn, Stonethwaite (017687 77239, CA12 5XG)
**NEARBY SWIM SPOTS:** There are multiple pool dipping opportunities in Stonethwaite and Langstrath Becks.

place so be prepared to share. It is pool beloved of adventurous local boys, mountaineers wishing to cool their aching limbs and a whole host of avid skinny dippers! It really is the Holy Grail of dub swimmers, and it has it all: deep crystal-clear water, a little waterfall, an easy to get into side, and a great side for 'joffing' (jumping off). My preference is to drop downstream a little further and swim upstream, trout-like, to the main body of the pool.

On a fine summer's day you could quite happily spend the whole day exploring this valley which also holds some of the finest climbing and scrambling in the county, to say nothing of the outstanding examples of flora and fauna hidden about the place. However, the avid pool hunter will be keen to get back to the pools of Galleny Force and the Fairy Glen ❹ once they have had their fill of the Pot. The lovely pools of Galleny Force are best accessed on the southern bank and are often in shade in the morning. Swimming the other pools on the return journey will give the always-hoped-for sun time to rise above Ullscarf and Eagle Crag to shine into all the dark corners

– something you may appreciate during a long day of dipping.

If you have the time, explore the woodland outcrops and crags along the way; there are some wonderfully airy scrambles en route and even a hidden bothy amongst the boulders. The legendary Woof Cave is extremely difficult to find and does not give up her secret easily! Whichever direction your rambles take you, you will have a wonderful day out, even with the notoriously wet Borrowdale weather. Remember to keep an eye out for wildlife, pack your binoculars and a large flask of tea and don't rush the experience.

### WEEKEND SUGGESTION

Camp or hostel it in Borrowdale or Buttermere and make the most of a long weekend in some of the finest countryside and swimming opportunities in Britain. Keswick is a short drive away and has a vibrant pub scene and some great fish and chip restaurants.

❶ Park at Rosthwaite and walk north, back up the B5289 a short way and turn right onto the track, signposted for Stonethwaite and the Hazelbank Hotel. Continue along the track and cross the bridge and turn right onto the Cumbria Way which crosses the road here. This is a nice level path with a wall to the left and Stonethwaite Beck on your right.

Stay on the Cumbria Way and continue through the gates and the corridor of hazels, the path becomes enclosed by walls before widening and opening up to some wonderful views towards the Borrowdale Fells. When you come to the right turn signed for Stonethwaite, continue straight on following the signpost for Grasmere on towards the looming Eagle Crag which dominates the skyline ahead.

Continue to follow the beck, ignoring the track on the left and continuing on the beckside path through gates and across open pastures. Pass through the water gate and over the bridge.

Remain on the path, passing the falls on the right, to Smithymire Island where Langstrath Beck joins Stonethwaite Beck, go through the gate on the right and over the footbridge making a dogleg to continue to follow the Cumbria Way up the eastern bank of Langstrath Beck.
**1.9 miles**

❷ After about a mile of walking in the shadow of Sergeant's Crag and nestled beneath a sheep fold, is Blackmoss Pot. Ford the beck above the Pot and walk back north for about 30 metres to access the swimming.
**1.2 miles**

**3** Return using the good track on the western bank of the beck, it is a very puddled but faster route than the eastern path and will take you back to the footbridge just under Bleak How. Ignore the footbridge again and follow the track through glades of hazel, oak and birch and, if you want to explore all that Langstrath has to offer, continue to follow the beck rather than taking the broad track that heads north-west once you are clear of the trees. This will bring you to the confluence of the Langstrath and Stonethwaite becks where there are some great little pools.

Continue to walk downstream of Stonethwaite Beck for a couple of hundred meters to get to a kink in the beck where you will find Galleny Force and its pools. There is a nice rocky corner to get changed on, or if it's a bit breezy, you can tuck in behind the nearby sheep fold. The pools directly beneath the falls are fun to explore but the lower-level pool downstream makes for a more satisfying and enjoyable short swim.
**1.2 miles**

**4** Return to Rosthwaite via the right of way that leads you through the campsite and the village of Stonethwaite. You'll pass by the very fine Langstrath Country Inn before walking back across Stonethwaite Bridge to return by the last short stretch of the Cumbria Way that you joined at the start of the walk.
**1.9 miles**

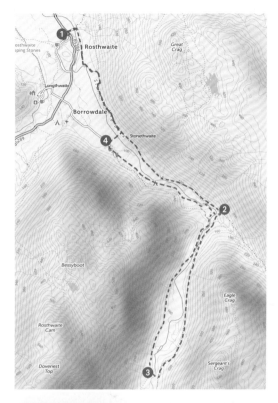

# Walk 11

# CASTLE CRAG, THE RIVER DERWENT AND MILLICAN DALTON'S CAVE

A walk packed with adventure, making it the perfect outing for a sunny summer's day.

*I*t is easy to travel by this vale of crystal pools, shallows and glides en route to the more obvious delights of the Buttermere valley, or the impressive open fellscapes of the Borrowdale valleys. However, on a sunny day a stroll up the Derwent is a real treat, and although you will no doubt meet many folk on your way, once you get past the campsite near Gowder Dub (a very popular swimming spot with the campers), you can often have the pick of the pools as walkers pass you by.

This route takes in the best that Grange and the surrounding area has to offer, including the marvellous summit viewpoint of Castle Crag, Millican Dalton's cave and some of the best river swimming in the Lakes.

Grange lies at the 'Jaws of Borrowdale', a dramatic narrowing of the terrain between Grange Fell and Castle Crag ❷, formed by glaciation and erosion. The hamlet originated in Medieval times when the monks of Furness Abbey built an outlying farm, or grange, here. The lovely double arched stone bridge crossing the River Derwent here was built in 1675 and is the defining feature of the place, along with the 18th-century churches (including the tiny, green slate Methodist church) and whitewashed cottages.

This small corner of Borrowdale is home to the lowest but surely the most picturesque Wainwright summit, Castle Crag, at 290 metres the only Wainwright to lie below 300 metres, yet the view is great. It and the surrounding woodland are places of beauty and are well-loved by all who visit. The war memorial on the summit is dedicated to the Borrowdale Valley men killed in World War I and a remembrance service takes place here every year on Remembrance Sunday.

*"If a visitor to Lakeland has only two or three hours to spare,*

## INFORMATION

DISTANCE: 5.3 miles
TIME: 5-6 hours
MAP: Harvey British Mountain Map: Lake District, OS Explorer OL4 The English Lakes NW
START/END POINT: The Bridge at Grange (NY 254 174)
PUBLIC TRANSPORT: Nearest train stations are Windermere or Penrith. From Windermere, take the 555 bus service to Keswick, from Penrith take the X5 or X4. From a Keswick take the 77a (April to October) or 78 bus service to Grange.
SWIMMING: Gowder Dub (NY 250 165), Stang Dub (NY 251 151), Pennybridge Dub (NY 253 155), Wilkinson's Dub (NY 253 162)
PLACES OF INTEREST: Millican Dalton's Cave, Bowder Stone, Watendlath, Ashness Bridge, Castle Crag, Holy Trinity Church at Grange.
REFRESHMENTS: Borrowdale Gates Hotel, Grange, offers excellent service and accommodation (017687 77204, CA12 5UQ). Grange Bridge Cottage Tea Shop, Grange, is perfectly situated near the river with a lovely garden in which to take tea (017687 77201, CA12 5UQ).
OTHER FACILITIES: Public toilets are situated next to the Grange Bridge Cottage Teashop.
ACCOMMODATION: Excellent accommodation at the Borrowdale Gates Hotel, Grange (017687 77204, CA12 5UQ). Very good campsite and B&B at Hollows Farm, Grange, Keswick (017687 77298, CA12 5UQ).

*poor fellow, yet desperately wants to reach a summit and take back an enduring memory of the beauty of the district...let him climb Castle Crag."*
A Wainwright

The old mine workings on the side of the crag, contain the summer residence of Millican Dalton, the self-proclaimed Professor of Adventure ❹. Millican Dalton lived in the cave here during the summer months for nearly 50 years. He spent his life outdoors and was almost entirely self-sufficient. He spent his days having adventures and guiding clients on rock climbing and mountaineering expeditions around the Lake District and abroad and was a real character and an exceptional mountaineer.

Millican was a loveable eccentric who made his own clothes and equipment, wore a Tyrolean hat and loved dark coffee and Woodbine cigarettes. He was considered very good campfire company and pioneered adventurous outdoor activities for women long before it was considered socially acceptable. The truest of gentlemen, he considered that a person's true spirit was forged in the crucible of adventure and I'm certain that he would approve of our swim-hiking route outlined here.

The Cumbria Way follows the river here along most of its course and all of the river pools, or dubs as we call them, make for wonderful swimming. Stang Dub, Pennybridge Dub, Wilkinson's Dub and Gowder Dub all have their own character and feature deep, clear pools set next to beaches of light slate pebble.

There are many ways in which you can vary the route outlined here – you can continue to Rosthwaite for lunch, float back down to Grange on an airbed or packraft, or just linger by your favourite pool. Have fun, but whatever you do, do it in the Spirit of Adventure!

## WEEKEND SUGGESTION

Camp at Hollows Farm or lush it up at The Borrowdale Gates and have a real holiday filled with adventure. This is a perfect Sunday day out, so perhaps fill Saturday with a visit to the Buttermere Valley for swimming and hill walking. Or spend a week exploring this exceptional part of the Lakes – run, climb scramble and swim. Keswick is a short drive away and has a vibrant pub scene and some great fish and chip restaurants too.

**1** Head into the village and past the two cafés around the corner. Take the first left down the tarmac road signposted 'Bridleway, Seatoller 3m, Rosthwaite 2m' heading south. Follow the road to the campsite, watching out for red squirrels along the way, and turn left at the junction signposted 'Castle Crag 1¾m'. Continue past the campsite on the left as the road turns into more of a farm track. Stay left as the track heads down towards the River Derwent and cross the wooden bridge, then continue straight on over another wooden bridge to Gowder Dub in the Derwent. This is a wonderful place to swim, but if you don't want to get wet just yet, this route does revisit it on the return journey.

The two bridges cross Broadslack Gill, follow the path that traces the gill south, south-west and gradually ascents towards Castle Crag. The path soon leads out of the woods, through a gate and on to the more open fellside, with Goat Crag and High Steel Knott looming over from the west. A small stone bridge crosses the gill and leads on to a cobbled track. The steep slate scree is visible from the old workings on Castle Crag to the east, just past the scree and before the col up ahead, take the path to the left that doubles back and steeply up a stepped path behind the scree.

Cross the stone stile and on up the steep but good path to another wall and gate. Stick to the path next to the wire fence and wall, until it meets another wall by two large

beech trees, heading north, north-east. This leads up to an impressive path that zig-zags up through the mass of slate scree towering above. Keep on ascending to the right, passing the quarry below and on to the small rocky summit, with memorial plaque, situated on a grassy plateau, studded with twisted larch. Enjoy the expansive views and then retrace your steps back to the cobbled track below.

**1.9 miles**

**2** For a shortened route, that would miss out Tongue Gill and Stang Dub, take the path that heads south, over the wooden stile spanning the wall on the descent from the summit, then east towards the river and Pennybridge Dub. Otherwise carry on down the steep summit path and back on to the cobbled track beneath and ascend to the col. Ignore the path that heads south, south-east down the fellside, and continue on the path that contours the fell and which follows the stone wall heading south, south-west. At the fork stay left until you reach Tongue Gill and its three wooden bridges.

Go through the gate in the fence and descend, staying close to the wire fence and track that follows the gill down and through a gate in the wall to the valley bottom. Here the gill from the left, and a wall from the right, funnel the walker into a tight corner, and a gate which leads over a small wooden bridge. The path continues to follow the gill to a gate and on to the main footpath

that is part of the Cumbria Way, and which follows the course of the River Derwent. Turn left on the broad track following the flow of the river, go over the wooden bridge that takes you, once again over Tongue Gill, and past the 'new' stone bridge. Pass through a gate and in a few meters, the river comes right by the track forming a deep glide up against a walled bank of the river. This is Stang Dub and is well worth a swim.

**1.2 miles**

**3** Continue on the Cumbria Way path, following the flow of the river due north. Where the path forks, follow the path next to the river to the woods ahead. Where the woods meet the river, the path crosses a stile and directly to Pennybridge Dub via a small scramble down the bank. The dub is very deep here and is contained by a pebble beach. Stay away from the current at the head of the pool, which pushes strongly into the steep bank, taking the unwary swimmer under.

Head back towards the stile where a gravel footpath is visible heading north through the woods, this is the Cumbria Way making its way back into the woods. Follow this path as it winds its way through the edge of the woods, gradually steering away from the river and begins to climb towards the quarry workings ahead. Eventually a stone wall cuts across the path from the steep ground to the west. Go through the gap in the wall and take the path left that follows the

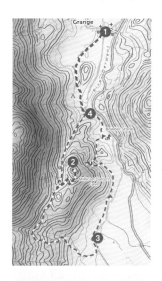

wall and up to the tiered slate workings above. This rather indistinct path eventually passes a rather dank, wet cave, before joining a good, gravelled path from the north which leads up to a small plateau, and the two open entrances of Millican Dalton's Cave. You will know you are in the right place if you see the words attributed to him carved into the stone near the entrance of the smaller opening: Don't waste Words, Jump to Conclusions.
**0.7 miles**

**4** From the cave, drop back onto the good path that heads north then winds east and which soon joins the main path through the woods. At a gap in the wall, turn right (east), and as the path bears north again, take the well-worn path east through the bracken to a small stand of larch, and Wilkinson's Dub. Here a long pebble beach borders the lively riffles that flow into the deep slow-flowing dub below.

From Wilkinson's Dub, head back to the main path and follow it until it reaches the river again at Gowder Dub where you can enjoy another swim before crossing the wooden bridges and heading back to Grange via the campsite.
**1.4 miles**

# CRUMMOCK WATER
# AND SCALE FORCE

This route around Crummock Water provides classic low-level walking with exceptional big lake swimming accessible along the way. Scale Force provides an interesting diversion.

Crummock Water is a distance swimmer's dream lake. Over 4 kilometres of quiet, clear lake to swim, no powerboats or steamers to worry about and flanked by the mighty fells of Grasmoor to the east and Mellbreak to the west, it takes some beating. A reasonable footpath contours most of the lake and although boggy in places, allows excellent access to the water. The proximity of Scale Force, with its ribbon-like falls and icy pool, offers an intimate distraction away from the big lake atmosphere.

The Lake District lakes and valleys were formed as the glaciers retreated during the last ice age 26,000 to 10,000 years ago. Looking at a plan view of a map of the Lakes, the valleys and lakes radiate outwards like the spokes of a wheel. Crummock Water is a perfect example of a ribbon lake formed by the retreat of the glaciers: it is deep and proportionately long and thin. Crummock and Buttermere were once one continuous lake, but over time deposits from Sourmilk Gill and Mill Beck divided it. Crummock Water measures up at 4km long, just under 1km wide and 43 metres deep, so there is plenty for the swimmer to explore in relative safety. The water it contains is very clear in all but the most turbulent conditions thanks to its rocky bottom and is used as a reservoir to supply the villages and towns of west Cumbria with water. It is well-protected by the National Trust as well as Nature England, who have banned any large-scale swimming events on the lake to prevent the risk of spreading non-native invasive species like the New Zealand pygmy weed that flourishes in nearby Derwentwater. This is the case for Buttermere and Wastwater too, and although these lakes provide the swimmer with near perfect swimming locations, we must be responsible for preserving the

## INFORMATION

**DISTANCE:** 9 miles
**TIME:** 6.5 hours
**MAP:** Harvey British Mountain Map: Lake District, OS Explorer OL4 The English Lakes NW
**START/END POINT:** National Trust Scale Hill Car Park (NY 149 215)
**PUBLIC TRANSPORT:** Nearest train stations are Windermere and Penrith. Buttermere is served by the number 77 bus from Keswick which has regular bus links with Penrith, Windermere and Workington stations.
**SWIMMING:** Crummock Water at Lanthwaite Wood (NY 152 208), Low Ling Crag (NY 157 183) and at Hause Point (NY 162 183). Scale Force (NY 151 172)
**PLACES OF INTEREST:** Honister Slate Mine, Buttermere Village, St James' Church
**REFRESHMENTS:** Kirkstile Inn, Loweswater (01900 85219, CA13 0RU); The Bridge Hotel, Buttermere (017687 70252, CA13 9UZ); Buttermere Court Hotel, Buttermere (017687 70253, CA13 9XA); Syke Farm Tea Room, Buttermere (017687 70277, CA13 9XA); Croft House Farm Café, Buttermere (017687 70235, CA13 9XA)
**EASIER ACCESS:** Buttermere has level access from the village.
**NEARBY SWIM SPOTS:** Along the entire shoreline of Crummock Water, Buttermere, River Derwent, Derwentwater, Loweswater

quality of the water here. Please note the advice given on biosecurity at the beginning of this book.

The main point of concern for the swimmer in Crummock is the changeable weather, the wind in particular. As for Buttermere, in certain weather conditions the shape of the surrounding fells funnels the wind onto the water, creating ferocious squalls and chop. However, on a calm day the surface is like glass and all around the lake the trout can be seen rising to the fly, dimpling the surface that reflects the fells above. Whatever the forecast, be prepared for changeable weather, it is part of the charm of the place and can add more than a dash of excitement to a swim (which not everyone appreciates). I had the privilege once of guiding a couple of charming ladies from London who wanted to swim the length of Crummock Water. A stiff breeze blew up creating some savage chop which really put them off their breast-stroke. They were regulars at the Serpentine in London and were really put out that there were waves to contend with and complained bitterly! I was forced to apologize for the vagaries of the weather and resorted to distracting them with jelly babies.

This route begins in the delightful Lanthwaite Woods which leads straight to the pebble beach where you can take in one of the best views of the lake. The sight of the clear water spreading out over the pebbles and onto the dramatic distant fells invites you to get in and swim. Why not start as you mean to go on and do just that. For the keen swim-hiker this is the perfect route to load up a tow-float with gear and swim most of the way, knowing that at any point, the path is but a stone's throw away.

The walk follows the rather boggy lake path anti-clockwise, beneath the towering mass of Mellbreak to one of the main features on the lakeshore, Low Ling Crag ❷. This curious spit of land juts out into the lake under High Ling Crag and forms a gravel peninsula with a craggy terminus. It is the perfect place for a picnic or a swim, or indeed both, before taking the steep path up to visit one of our highest waterfalls.

Scale Force ❸ emanates from a deep re-entrant between Starling Dodd and Red Pike and at 38 metres is the highest single-drop waterfall in the district. It is not at all impressive from the little bridge that leads to the outflow and to fully appreciate its charm you need to scramble up the slippery rocks to its base. Its not an easy route, but a confident hill walker used to Lake District scrambles will take it in their stride. The pool at the base is always delightfully cold, which along with the down blast of air from the falls, takes the breath of any valiant swimmer away.

Buttermere village ❹ offers a number of ways to refresh oneself en route to the eastern side of the lake and if you can make it past the pubs and the excellent ice cream parlour at Sykes Farm, your reward will be stunning views of Crummock from a new perspective. The hike up and over Rannerdale Knotts ❺ gives a bird's eye view of the lake and used to be the original route to the village before the shoreside road was built and leads to Cinderdale.

Cinderdale Common is named after the ancient bloomeries which were primitive furnaces where iron was smelted from local ore. The product was a mass of iron and slag (or cinders) called blooms. The pleasant grassy path that crosses the common, leads once more to the path next to the lake, and eventually back to the woods at Lanthwaite. This bit of shoreline presents more ideal places to get in for a swim and is much more pleasant to walk than the boggy tracks of the west side of the lake. The final stretch leads you through woods of birch, beech, larch, spruce and some impressive Scot's pine and provides a fitting end to a first-rate walk.

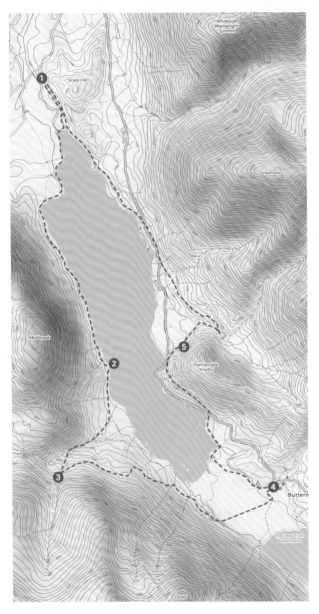

**1** From the car park walk south, south-east through the woods for 600 metres towards the lake and the crescent-shaped gravel beach which looks along the length of the Crummock. Head south-west past the stone waterworks buildings and over the River Cocker via the bridge to the shoreline path.

Stay on the path over Park Beck and on past the pump house and around the bulbous peninsula that was once the site of an ancient pele tower, with a twin moat that protected locals from marauding Scots. Stay on the path all the way as it takes you to the west of the lake and continues on its south, south-easterly direction, beneath Mellbreak. From here, navigation is simple. Just follow the shore for about 2 kilometres to Low Ling Crag peninsula and perhaps wring your socks out and take a break from bog trotting.
**2.2 miles**

**2** The route to Scale Force takes the path that heads directly south from Low Ling for about 500 metres. Take the right fork in the path heading south-east which follows one of the many branches of the mini delta emanating from Scale Beck. On reaching Scale Beck proper, carry on up the valley to a fork in the path, take the left fork over the footbridge and continue up by Scale Beck and up to the re-entrant that it has formed.

A small wooden footbridge marks the entrance to the outflow of the falls. To get a reasonable view of

Scale Force it is necessary to scramble up past the small fall in the foreground. To take an even closer look at the force and perhaps take a dip in the pool at its base, press on up the slippy rocks by the side of the beck. Take care here; although the rocks are slippery, the hand and footholds are all there and all it takes is a methodical approach to scramble up to the next level. The pool is accessed by clambering over the fallen trees and leaping the pools until a small gravel beach is reached, giving good access to the water. Please remember that this is a unique wild place, treat it with respect and do no damage.
**0.9 miles**

❸ From the footbridge at Scale Force, follow the path that heads north-east and travels a short way down the fell, before contouring around to the east to join the main lakeshore path at Ruddy Beck. After about 600 metres, take the path that crosses Buttermere Dubs over the farm bridge heading east, north-east. After traversing the fields, the path emerges onto a farm track which zig-zags into Buttermere village.

Walk past the Buttermere Court Hotel (formerly The Fish) and take the sharp left that takes you past the campsite, public toilets and pay and display car park.
**1.9 miles**

❹ At the end of the car park the path continues, following Mill Beck all the way to the south end of Crummock. At the edge of the lake

turn right and follow the path over the footbridge heading north-east for 100 metres, then turn north-west and up through the woods, following the shoreline all the way to the B5289 road.

Cross the road and take the path immediately opposite which heads on up the side of the fell in a north-westerly direction. This takes you under Rannerdale Knotts, giving excellent views over Hause Point and out over to Low Ling Crag. Descend down to the small car park at the base of the slope. This gives good access to a small bay on the other side of the road, popular with swimmers and divers alike.
**1.4 miles**

❺ From the car park follow the path by the wall heading north-east. After 500 metres the path leaves the wall and trends south-east leading up the valley to cross Squat Beck by the bridge. Heading north-west, stay on the path all the way to the rough car park and road at Cinderdale Common.

250 metres on from the car park, cross the road and go through the gate and pick up the lakeshore footpath once more and follow it roughly north-west through the pines at High Wood, past the National Trust boathouse and on to Lanthwaite Wood and the end of our walk.
**2.6 miles**

# Walk 13

# BLEABERRY TARN, HIGH STILE AND BUTTERMERE

The Buttermere fells are considered by many, including Wainwright, to be the most beautiful. The tarns and lakes here mirror that beauty and offer unsurpassed swimming opportunities.

The great circle of mountains surrounding Buttermere were among Wainwright's favourite, and his ashes were scattered by Innominate Tarn up on Haystacks. At St James's Church in Buttermere there is a memorial to Wainwright, and one can see Haystacks from the window.

For a man who knew the Lakes as well as Wainwright to choose this as his final resting place says a lot about the attraction of this place and its fells. Add to that the fact that Buttermere has the clearest water of all of the Lake District lakes, and you have the grounds for an exceptional day of hiking and swimming. Although extremely popular, one can never tire of exploring Buttermere and its mountains.

The route up to Red Pike ❸ from Buttermere is one of the most popular in the valley despite the steep climb. The traverse of Red Pike, High Stile ❹ and High Crag ❺ is a classic fell-walking route. The scar of Sour Milk Gill carves a line straight down through Birkness Woods, flowing almost as one continuous waterfall and draws the eye up towards Dodd which obscures Red Pike from the valley floor. The path adjacent to it offers the quickest route up onto the magnificent ridge of fell tops which dominate this side of the Buttermere valley which also happens to hide the best swimming tarn in the valley.

Bleaberry Tarn ❷ nestles in the high cirque beneath Red Pike. It is one of a series of hanging valleys running along the ridge, including Ling and Birkness Combes, features left by the ice ages that also carved the attractive ribbon lakes below. Very early guidebooks suggested it was part of ancient volcano, but it is a cirque

## INFORMATION

DISTANCE: 7.1 miles
TIME: 6 hours
MAP: Harvey British Mountain Map: Lake District, OS Explorer OL4 The English Lakes NW
START/END POINT: Buttermere Car Park (NY 172 169), next to the Buttermere Court Hotel, CA13 9XA
PUBLIC TRANSPORT: Buttermere Village is served by The Honister Rambler 77/77A bus service from Keswick. There are regular bus links to Keswick from Penrith, Windermere and Workington stations and occasionally from Carlisle.
SWIMMING: Bleaberry Tarn (NY 166 154), Buttermere (NY 184 153)
PLACES OF INTEREST: Honister Slate Mine (CA12 5XN), Buttermere Village, St James' Church, Whinlatter Forest Park (for picnics, Go Ape and mountain biking)
REFRESHMENTS: Kirkstile Inn, Loweswater (01900 85219, CA13 0RU); The Bridge Hotel, Buttermere (017687 70252, CA13 9UZ); Buttermere Court Hotel, Buttermere (017687 70253, CA13 9XA); Syke Farm Tea Room, Buttermere (017687 70277, CA13 9XA); Croft House Farm Café (017687 70277, CA13 9XA)
EASIER ACCESS: Buttermere has level access to the lake from the village.
NEARBY SWIM SPOTS: Crummock Water, River Derwent, Derwentwater, Loweswater

tarn set in splendid isolation between Red Pike and High Stile which loom above.

Bleaberry is the local term for Bilberry which grew much more profusely on the Cumbria fells before sheep farming became so widespread. Sheep graze on the young shoots holding back plant growth, but you can still find patches growing where the sheep can't get at them. The leaves can be used to make a tea to relieve upset stomachs, and the berries picked in early autumn to eat and to make dye. They provide a tasty alfresco treat if ever you come across them.

The tarn itself is just under 6 metres deep, the deepest part being at the inflow. It has a very steep west and south-east shore with more of a gradual drop off to the north-west. This information becomes more relevant when the state of the tarn floor is revealed. It is made of the sharpest and most awkward rock imaginable. If you have been sensible enough to bring along some light footwear to swim in, then take the gradual route into the water. If going barefoot, the steeper shoreline will offer a more abrupt entry into the chilly water but will, no doubt, be less painful. The water appears dark and uninviting in all but the brightest weather and the sun only reaches it in the warmer months, but the water is crystal clear and refreshing to swim in after the steep climb up.

The walk up to The Saddle, the col which links Dodd with Red Pike is the best way to warm up after a cold mountain swim and leads to one of the finest ridge walks in the Lakes. The view down the north-east side of the ridge is unsurpassed. One can easily visualise the action of the two vast glaciers that carved out the Warnscale and Gatesgarth valleys joining forces to form one long trench that eventually became Buttermere and Crummock as the glacier continued on its way to the Solway Firth. The great spur of Fleetwith Pike was left in their wake and this feature has come to define the spectacular views of Buttermere from the north-west. To the south can be seen Scoat Fell, Pillar, Kirk Fell and Great Gable and if it weren't for the siren call of the shimmering blue lake below, one could spend the whole day walking to the horizon.

*"Scarth Gap is one of the pleasantest of the foot passes… the gradients are gentle and the view both ahead and behind are full of interest."* A Wainwright, *The Western Fells*

Scarth Gap Pass ❻ links the Buttermere valley with Ennerdale, and I have always associated it with climbing expeditions to Pillar and with merry nights spent at the Black Sail Hut eating mountains of their famous curry after long days on the fell. It provides a pleasant descent route from the ridge to reach Buttermere ❼. After having spent the best part of the morning gazing longingly down at the water it is good to finally reach it and get a good swim in.

The larch copse at Horse Close provides a good base to take a break from the hiking and have a picnic, and offers some good swimming options. The Buttermere Pines, along with some handsome beech, larch and ash, lie opposite at Hassness Point which is a 300 metre swim away. The pines are Scots pines, a native of the once extensive Caledonian pine forests and our only native pine tree. Ships masts were one of their many uses and you can appreciate why when you see then grouped together. Here they are famous enough to have their own name and have been extensively photographed. The swim over to Hassness Point is not too daunting and the blue slate shingle beaches beneath the pines are a nice place to linger on a sunny day.

Char Cottage, the little white hut, forlorn in the meadow beneath Fleetwith Pike, is probably the most coveted property in the Lakes. Forget Mil-

lionaire's Row on the shores of Windermere, what one would give to live here! The deep bay in front of the cottage offers some unique swimming in an unbeatable location. The last time I swam here, a crew were filming Tom Cruise in a helicopter, while black clad parascenders swept down from High Crag; they were filming the next *Mission Impossible* film and were causing quite a stir in the valley. Their safety crew, riding sleek electric jet skis were very friendly and accommodating and allowed us to swim in the bay as long as we 'stayed out of shot'.

The history of the tiny Char Cottage is uncertain, but it was no doubt used as a site for char fishing. The Arctic char is a glacial relict fish, which means that it is a species that originates from the time after the last glacial period approximately 12,000 years ago. In England they are only found in the Lake District and used to be fished commercially. A small handful of locals still fish for them here, their fishing grounds, and techniques are a closely guarded secret. If you are early enough on the lake you can watch them fish. Look out for stooped old men in well-kept rowing boats, with two long bowed rods fixed port and starboard from which they troll the handmade silver lures attached to the line.

The inflow from Warnscale Beck creates long, swirling gravel bars as it enters the lake and brings frigid water in from the Warnscale catchment. The beck is a very special environment and is home to unusual river plants that I have never seen anywhere else. Although very shallow in places, it is worth a gentle explore into the deeper pools just for the experience of seeing what grows there. Take care not to disturb anything and bear in mind that you are swimming within a Site of Special Scientific Interest (SSSI).

Even during the summer, the water here can be quite cool and a return to shore and to warm, dry clothes becomes pressing. The return route to the village is a pleasant walk along the south-western wooded shoreline and offers even more swimming if the mood takes you. Once back at Buttermere, there are a limited number of refreshment options, but rest assured that they are all very good. The author would recommend one of Syke Farm's excellent ice creams, or brandy and hot chocolate in The Bridge depending on the season. If your eye is drawn once more towards Hay Stacks, perhaps keep an eye out for the benevolent spirit of Wainwright, or even Ethan Hunt descending in a parachute.

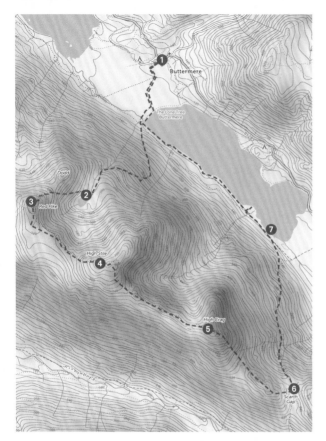

Once out of the woods the path heads directly up the fell for 200 metres before zig-zagging then traversing west towards Sourmilk Gill. Remain on the south-east side of the path and after a few hundred meters the terrain levels out onto broad moraine where the path passes over the outflow leading directly to Bleaberry Tarn.

The water from the north-west shore deepens gradually in contrast to the steep shelving south-east shore.
**1.5 miles**

❷ From the outflow of the tarn, follow the path which initially heads north-west, veering to the west as it cuts across the fell to the saddle linking Red Pike with Dodd. Once on The Saddle, the path continues west as it zig-zags up the rocky spur directly to the summit cone and cairn of Red Pike.
**0.4 miles**

❸ From Red Pike descend south on the rocky path for 300 metres before it bears south-east and follows the level ridgeline towards the rocky cone of High Stile ahead. As the path steepens it backs to the east for 200 metres before the summit of High Stile at 806 metres. Pedants will be duty-bound to take the short detour to the official height point of 807 metres a short way along the north-east spur before they can claim the summit.
**0.7 miles**

❶ From the car park, walk around the Buttermere Court Hotel (previously The Fish). Go through the gate and follow the track past the Buttermere Court Hotel car park where the track veers off in a dogleg to the left. Follow the track to the hedged-in track, ignoring the path that leads off to the right towards Scale Bridge. The hedged-in track zig-zags before heading straight for the lake. Pass through the gate and turn right and walk along the edge of the meadow to the footbridge over Buttermere Dubs. Head roughly south, past the footbridge 40 metres up from the river which spans Sourmilk Gill (stay to the left of it) and pick up the steep path (still heading just east of south) that leads diagonally across the fell through the woods.

**4** From High Stile (the 806 metre summit) head off the summit cone bearing east, south-east and follow the path atop the long, dramatic ridgeline above Comb Crags. After just over a kilometre the route heads east before the gentle ascent to High Crag.
**1 mile**

**5** From High Crag descend steeply down Gamlin End to the broad col below. Pass the tarnlet there before carrying on up the gradual slope up to Seat. Stay on the ridge heading south-east until the route turns to the east and drops steeply down to the col at Scarth Gap.
**0.7 miles**

**6** Take the descent route to the left at Scarth Gap, heading due north down the pass. Stay on the good path of the Scarth Gap Pass as it crosses Warnscale and eventually meets and follows a wall just after High Wax Knott. Stay on the path, continuing this long descent, as it heads north all the way to the Buttermere shoreline path just along from Peggy's Bridge.
**1.1 miles**

**7** Follow the shore path along the south-west shore of Buttermere all the way back to the bridge at Buttermere Dubs. The swimming is good all the way along this shoreline although Horse Close provides a good base. From Buttermere Dubs bridge retrace the route back to the village to finish.
**1.7 miles**

# Walk 14

# STICKLE TARN AND
# THE LANGDALE PIKES

A straightforward and popular route, with dramatic
swims and the option of some scrambling.

*G*reat Langdale Valley – a sweeping and majestic
gateway to adventure! Every time I take the journey
on the single, winding road into Langdale I feel like
I'm coming home; or rather, the place I would always
prefer to be. There is so much to explore here as the
valley is a great big glacially-carved place crenelated
with some of the best crags in the Lakes and dotted with remote
tarns, secret dubs and hidden pools at the feet of tumbling falls
that only a rare few have set eyes upon considering the popularity
of the dale. It is also home to the best pub in England, the Old
Dungeon Ghyll, or 'The Old' to her friends. Crucially for the
mountain swimmer, The Old has that most essential of country
pub features, a perpetually roaring fire.

This is a very straightforward and popular route, with some
interesting variations involving two classic scrambling routes. We
will stick to the standard route in this description, but I would
urge anyone with a taste for the steeps to bring along a copy of
the Cicerone *Scrambles in the Lake District – South* and customise
this route to their own liking.

The route up Stickle Gill ❶ is best taken with a steady
Himalayan plod as it is rather steep, though never a slog. The
surrounding falls, pools and excellent views across the valley do
a great job of distracting you from the hard work and before you
know it you are peering over the edge of the small dam wall and
into the clear water of Stickle Tarn. Framed by the Langdale Pikes,
this has got to be one of the most dramatic swims in Cumbria and
it is a relief, even on a cool day, to slip into the cold peaty water
after the steep climb.

The Langdale Pikes provide the defining feature of Great
Langdale and include Pike of Stickle, Loft Crag, Harrison Stickle
and Pavey Ark, and are all situated along a ridge on the northern

## INFORMATION

DISTANCE: 3.1 miles
TIME: 3 hours walking, 1 hour swimming
MAP: Harvey British Mountain Map:
Lake District, OS Explorer OL6 The
English Lakes SW
START/END POINT: The car park at
New Dungeon Ghyll (NY 295 064
PUBLIC TRANSPORT: Nearest train
station is Windermere. Bus services
are the 555 bus service that runs
between Windermere and Keswick via
Ambleside. From Ambleside take the
516 bus to Great Langdale.
SWIMMING: Stickle Tarn (NY 287 077).
PLACES OF INTEREST: Pike of Stickle
Neolithic Axe Factory (NY 274 072).
REFRESHMENTS: New Dungeon
Ghyll Hotel, Ambleside (015394
37213, LA22 9JX); Sticklebarn ,
Ambleside (015394 37356, LA22 9JU);
The Old Dungeon Ghyll Hotel,
Ambleside (015394 37272, LA22 9JY)
OTHER FACILITIES: Public toilets are
situated next to the Sticklebarn pub.
ACCOMMODATION: Good
accommodation is to be found at any
of the 3 pubs/hotels in the valley noted
under Refreshments. Herdy Huts offer
romantic shepherd hut accommodation
which is a nice change from the norm
and come highly recommended
(herdyhuts.co.uk). There is also a
bunkhouse at Stickleburn and two good
campsites: Baysbrown Farm Campsite
(015394 37150, LA22 9JZ), National
Trust Great Langdale Campsite
(015394 32733, LA22 9JU).
NEARBY SWIM SPOTS: There are
multiple mountain pool dipping
opportunities in Stickle Gill and
Dungeon Gill.

side of the dale. They present a formidable sight from the valley floor but once on the ridgeline the gentle sweep of the terrain up towards High Raise becomes apparent and makes for some wonderful fell walking providing some of the best views in the South Lakes.

Stickle Tarn ❷ lies in the large corrie beneath Harrison Stickle and Pavey Ark, it is a natural tarn that was enlarged by the building of a stone dam in 1838 to provide water for Millbeck mill as well as for the gunpowder works at Elterwater. Thankfully, the dam does not detract from the drama of the place and as it raised the tarn depth by a couple of metres, provides us with more water to swim in which is nice. The tarn still supplies drinking water to the homes and businesses beneath – so don't wee in the water! There is a sheep track most of the way around the tarn but wherever you decide to get in for a swim, make sure you position yourself to take in the fantastic view of Pavey Ark, one of the best climbing crags in Cumbria and an awesome backdrop for a swim.

For those short on time (or wanting to make a day of the tarn swimming opportunity), you could just descend the same way following your swim, and the gill provides some very classy pool dipping during the descent. However, some of the finest hillwalking in Lakeland lies ahead and it would be a shame to miss it. As well as the great walking the views down from the ridgeline of the pikes provide excellent aerial views of Stickle Tarn and the valley bottom and gives a grand perspective to the ripples you have just left below. After exploring Harrison Stickle and taking in the views, those seeking the opportunity to stand amongst ancient history may want to take a detour to the Pike of Stickle axe factory. On the south-eastern side of Pike of Stickle, Neolithic workers quarried and roughly shaped the volcanic 'greenstone' rock into blanks that used to be traded the length and breadth of the country. Otherwise, the descent via Loft Crag follows a broad spur, is relatively easy on the legs and has the glittering form of Dungeon Gill flowing to the north-east side of it.

*...If ever you to Langdale go;*
*Into a chasm a mighty block*
*Hath fallen, and made a bridge of rock:*
*The gulf is deep below;*
*And, in a basin black and small,*
*Receives a lofty waterfall...*

William Wordsworth, 'The Idle Shepherd Boys'

This is a spectacular gill and provides some classic scrambling and it is worth taking a look into it when the gradient of the spur eases off. The culminating fall of Dungeon Gill Force, a 60-foot waterfall, immortalised in William Wordsworth's poem 'The Idle Shepherd Boys', is certainly worth a look and provides some nice pools to cool your feet in following the descent.

## WEEKEND SUGGESTION

Book yourself a 3-night stay in a Herdy Hut and walk your socks off. If you have the energy there are two more excellent swimming walks based in the Great Langdale valley that you simply must do and the pubs and eccentric locals will provide excellent evening entertainment. Ambleside is only a 20 minute drive away and has good restaurants, cafés and cinemas.

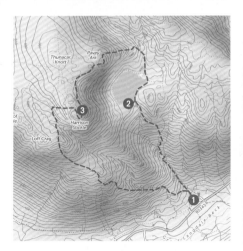

❶ Take the footpath that leads straight up the fell side behind the Sticklebarn pub, following the cascading course of Stickle Gill. Once past the footbridge 300 metres from the start, there are paths on both sides of the gill, but stick to the left and prepare yourself for a steep hike up one of the most dramatic walking routes in the Lakes. Just follow Stickle Gill all the way and after a kilometre and over 400 metres of ascent you will arrive at the small dam wall at Stickle Tarn.
**0.6 miles**

❷ Take the footpath that leads you almost directly north from the north-east corner of the tarn for about 300 metres before heading north-west on an ascending path that follows Bright Beck. This path curves around to the left and away from the beck onto easy terrain, eventually horseshoeing around to the cairn that marks the top of

Pavey Ark. The adventurous can take a short cut to this point by ascending Jack's Rake from the tarn, an easy but very exposed scramble that slashes the face of Pavey Ark and provides an exhilarating shortcut to the top (Ref: *Scrambles in the Lake District – South*, a guidebook by Cicerone).

After you have enjoyed the aerial view of the tarn, skirt around the gullies and scree above the tarn following the path first west, south-west away from the cairn, then after 100 metres or so just past the tarnlets, change direction to the south-west for 50 metres, before resuming its west, south west course above the steep ground atop the crags below. The path soon bears around to the south towards Harrison Stickle, always following the edge of the steep slope to the crags. Harrison Stickle is a very prominent feature in good visibility and the path

skirts around its eastern side before the scramble to the high point at 736 metres.
**1.2 miles**

❸ After exploring the Stickle and more fine views over Great Langdale Valley, head north, north-west for 100 metres and take the path that heads west, then south and south-east following the broad spur descending steeply from Loft Crag at first, before levelling out as it descends. This path leads right back to the car park at the New Dungeon Ghyll. This descent can be made even more interesting by going off the grid a little and exploring the Dungeon Gill (another excellent scrambling route) with its steep dungeon like walls and enclosed waterfalls, which culminates in Dungeon Gill Force, hidden in the trees not far off the footpath. Continue down the path to the hotels and car park to finish.
**1.2 miles**

# YEW TREE TARN, THE HOLME FELL TARNS AND HODGE CLOSE QUARRY

Interesting, easy-going walking through lovely terrain within easy reach of Ambleside and Coniston, featuring some unique swimming venues, each with its own charm.

This is a very accessible walk that usually doesn't get too busy, even during the summer months. It takes in some lovely swimming spots and some fine, often overlooked fell walking. All of the swimming locations have their own unique appeal, and the return walk offers the opportunity of an extension for more swimming in nearby High Arnside Tarn and Tarn Hows.

Conveniently there is parking in the lay-bys right next to Yew Tree Tarn ❶ and more parking further down the A593 road towards Coniston if you didn't get up early enough to bag a space. The tarn here is a lovely sight, marred only by its location next to the busy road, but it offers a convenient and rather pretty start to a walk that always offers more that the sum of its parts.

Yew Tree Tarn is named for the farm down the road, once owned by our cherished Beatrix Potter, who worked in close partnership with the newly established National Trust to help the existing farm tenants develop their tea shop and farming business as well as protect the estate for future generations to enjoy. Yew Tree Farm still thrives on many levels and produces excellent heritage meat from their Herdwick sheep and Belted Galloway cattle herds, whom you will no doubt meet during this walk.

The presence of a small dam wall at its southern end reveals the tarn is artificial. Depending on the water level, it can offer a very picturesque place to swim, although it is always shallow, never more than a metre in depth. It was created by James Garth Marshall of Monk Coniston in the 1930s who dammed Yewdale Beck to form a fishing lake. It is still operated as such today by the Coniston & Torver Angling Association, although the fluctuating water levels hamper the survival rates of the poor trout. Marshall

## INFORMATION

**DISTANCE:** 3.6 miles
**TIME:** 3 hours
**MAP:** Harvey British Mountain Map: Lake District, OS Explorer OL7 The English Lakes SE
**START/END POINT:** Yew Tree Tarn Layby Parking (NY 322 003)
**PUBLIC TRANSPORT:** Nearest train station is Windermere. Take the 555 bus service to Ambleside then a taxi to Yew Tree Tarn (15 minutes).
**SWIMMING:** Yew Tree Tarn (NY 321 004), Holm Fell Tarn (NY 316 011), Hodge Close Quarry (NY 317 017)
**PLACES OF INTEREST:** Cathedral Quarry, Brantwood House, The Ruskin Museum, The Steam Yacht Gondola, Peel Island on Coniston Water, The Armitt Museum in Ambleside, Zeffirellis Restaurant and Cinema
**REFRESHMENTS:** Swallows and Amazons Tearoom at Bank Ground Farm, something for everyone and great food on the east side of the Coniston Water (015394 41264, LA21 8AA). The Bluebird Café, Coniston (015394 41649, LA21 8AN); there are many more cafés, restaurants and pubs in both Coniston and Ambleside.
**EASIER ACCESS:** There is a car park at Hodge Close Quarry – access to the water still requires skill, but this eliminates the walking.
**NEARBY SWIM SPOTS:** Grasmere, Rydal Water, Coniston Water.

Wainwright rates Holme Fell as "one of the most attractive of Lakeland's fells" and it offers the most comprehensive panoramic fell-top viewing diagram there is, which will be of interest to those who like to understand their view. There are some 37 fells which can be viewed from Holme Fell summit and most can also be seen from the Gap including Pike O Blisco, Harrison's Stickle, High Raise, Helvellyn, Dollywagon Pike, Fairfield and Red Screes to name but a few. To take in all this and then notice the glimmer of tarns no more than a few hundred meters away is balm to the soul of the swim-hiker.

The Holme Fell Tarns ❷ (actually old reservoirs that used to supply water to the slate mines at Hodge Close Quarry) provide an intimate place to swim in the middle of the rambling jumble of fell covered with bog asphodel, bilberry, cotton grass, heather, juniper and bracken. The largest of the tarns, and the only one worth swimming in, is surrounded by alder, pine and birch and has a raised craggy feature which overlooks the water, providing an ideal place to picnic and dry off post-swim. The smaller tarn, about 50 metres to the west is worth a look just out of interest, but is shallow (less that a metre), murky with a sharp rocky bottom and is no pleasure to swim in, in marked contrast to the larger tarn.

Holme Fell Tarn is a hard place to leave behind, but more exciting swimming lies but half a mile away. A short walk through the woods and some ancient slate workings lead to Hodge Close Quarry ❸. This is one of many slate workings in the Tilberthwaite Valley which lies between Langdale and Coniston. The quarry was active from the early 19th century up until the 1960s and now provides an exciting location for extreme diving, climbing and outdoor swimming. It is

was also the driving force behind the 'landscape improvements' which led to the damming of Tarn Hows which was originally three much smaller tarns (Low Tarn, Middle Tarn and High Tarn) and is now one of the most popular and visited places in the Lakes.

The walk through the oak and birch woodland surrounding the tarn leads to a fantastic stand of Douglas fir which dominates the northern end of the tarn. Here the path cuts up through rough fell, sparsely populated by mixed woodland, occasional crags and large boulders. This must be one of the most rewarding short ascents in Lakeland, perhaps even on a par with Castle Crag in Borrowdale. Cresting the apex of Uskdale Gap offers a most spectacular view which makes the spirit soar, even in the most miserable of Lake District weather.

worth pointing out early on that the swimming here in itself is completely safe, it is the getting to the water that can be the tricky part! On entering the quarry, one assumes that caution, safety and common sense will be the priority, inexperienced divers and climbers have perished here, so please try not to add to the death toll. The reward for such diligence will be an unforgettable swimming experience in what seems on first impressions to be a beautiful dystopian hinterland.

The light-green coloured slate so prized by the slate men lends the water a viridescent hue that we swimmers always find so irresistible. The attraction is augmented by the thin waterfall at the northern end which fans out into spray as it hits the vast, sheer sides of the quarry walls and into the water beneath.

There are three ways into the quarry. One necessitates a bit of climbing: it can be intimidating, but the hand and footholds are all there if you just face into the rock and look. The opening in the protective wire fence leads to a scramble onto the scree below (in heavy rain this can be a little waterfall). The steep scree trod leads steeply down into the quarry and splits. The path to the left leads to a terrace with another short scramble down to a slim beach, the right path descends into bouldery scree which continues straight down into the clear water.

Another way in takes the most exciting route through a tunnel reached by a little path just north-west of the car park, but which involves a few hundred meters of wading the stream in the tunnel then a climb down a fixed ladder to the scree below. Divers often use this route as they come pre-prepared with dry suits and headlamps. Our route takes the third option which is the safest and most straightforward, but even this way in is

far from boring. The first glimpse of the water through the big archways in the dark quarry wall is thrilling.

The water in the quarry is deep and often cold, there are no shallows and there may be discarded metal anywhere in the water. It is not a place for poor swimmers or unsupervised children. It goes without saying that care must be taken when getting in and before attempting any jumping into the water. If you plan to jump in from the ledges in the quarry and explore the caves, please be careful and pack a small waterproof first aid kit, a tow float, a helmet, wetsuit shoes and a headtorch. Safety warnings aside, there is still plenty to explore safely here, and it is a wonderful place in which to spend time.

Once you have had your fill of Hodge Close, the walk back across High Oxen Fell offers pleasant, easy walking along the farm track and gives more great views towards Grasmere Common and the Langdales. The track soon reaches the main A593 road which links Ambleside to Coniston, and the path that runs alongside the road makes for a pleasant return route.

At Oxen Fell High Cross (at the beginning of stage 4 in the directions below) an extension to the walk can be made by crossing the road and following the road/track that forms part of the Cumbria Way. It leads past High Arnside Tarn, which is a little overgrown but good for a dip, and on to Tarn Hows. A return to the start can be made by descending from Tarn Hows via Tom Gill and back along the footpath in the woods that follows the road.

All in all, this is an adventure-packed little route within easy travelling distance from the accommodation hubs of Ambleside and Coniston and with all of the amenities they offer.

**1** From the lay-by car park next to Yew Tree Tarn head around to the southern end of the tarn, crossing the dam and following the footpath around the western shoreline. As the tarn is so shallow, swimming is best done from this shoreline where it is at its deepest.

Carry on along the path to the grove of Douglas fir and head off to the north-west to find the gate in the wall. Follow the path that cuts diagonally to the south-west through Harry Guards Wood. As the path steepens it meets another path at a T-junction, turn right on to the path towards the big boulders ahead. The path steepens as it leads through sparse mixed woodland and follows a thin gill flowing down from the Uskdale Gap above. Follow the path as it becomes less steep and passes between a broad cleft in the fellside which soon opens out

onto the Uskdale Gap; a flat col between two rocky outcrops. Step over the ancient tumbledown wall and admire the view.

Holme Fell Tarn can be seen from the Gap, follow the well-worn path down through the attractive bogland below to get to the tarn. The easiest place to get in to swim is at the northern end of the tarn.
**0.9 miles**

**2** Re-join the path from the north shore heading north, north-east. The path passes through some old slate buildings in the woods just as it becomes covered in loose slate. This path soon meets a broad track at a T-junction, turn right and follow the track to the gate and carry on through the woods. Follow the track by the gill and the wall to another gate, and just to its left, a stile in the fence. Go over the stile and walk the short

distance to the edge of Hodge Close Quarry.

The nearest edge of the quarry from this path provides alternative access into the maw of the quarry via a short climb. Go through the opening in the protective wire fence to start the scramble down (see above for detailed scrambling directions).

My recommendation is to ignore this way down and continue walking on the path to the road. Turn right at the road and follow it past the car park and between the big boulders for 300 metres to the old quarry buildings at Hodge Close Cottage and the bunkhouse where the road forms a tight zig-zag. Just past this kink in the road there is a track signed for High Oxen Fell. Follow this track and after about 30 metres, and just before the gate, turn right and follow the thin path through another gap in the protective fence which leads steeply down a rock- and scree-covered path to two arched open tunnels in the quarry wall ahead. These rock archways lead to short, but direct drops into the water. The archway offering the safest access to the water is the one with the old iron crane tracks which lead to the edge. Remember to always check the water before you jump.

A swim to the right (the western shore) leads to a thin gravel beach which allows good access to the rocky tunnels that cannot be seen from the get in point.
**0.6 miles**

**3** Retrace your steps up out of the quarry to the track that was signposted for High Oxen Fell. Turn right (east) onto the track and go through the gate and follow the road next to the small, almost grown-over tarn. Keep going and carry on through another gate in a wall, past a little outcrop of juniper and down the zig-zag road and over the beck. Carry on through the gate at the farm to pass through the farmyard and keep going on what is now a road. Pass the small open barn and stay right at the fork in the road until the main A593 road is reached.
**0.9 miles**

**4** Just before the main road, there is a footpath that runs alongside it to the right. Access this path via the kissing gate and stay on this path all the way back to Yew Tree Tarn, ignoring the gates in the wall leading off the path. Just before the tarn is reached, go through the 5 bar gate in the wall and take the footbridge over Yewdale Beck. Ignore the track to the gate in the wall and instead follow the small path of stepping stones that cross the boggy ground at the northern end of the tarn. Follow this path around the eastern shore of the tarn and back to the car park lay-by.
**1.2 miles**

# SOUR MILK GILL, EASEDALE AND CODALE TARNS

A popular walk that goes one step further, taking the adventure swimmer to the solitude of Codale Tarn.

## INFORMATION

DISTANCE: 6.2 miles
TIME: 5 hours walking, 1-2 hours swimming.
MAP: Harvey's British Mountain Map: Lake District, OS Explorer OL7 & OL6 for Codale Tarn.
START/END POINT: Heaton Cooper Studios, Grasmere (NY 336 075, LA22 9SX)
PUBLIC TRANSPORT: Nearest train station is Windermere. The 555 and 599 bus services run from Windermere.
PARKING: Grasmere village, also Grasmere Primary School, Stock Lane, LA22 9SJ (it's inexpensive and all the proceeds go to the development of the school).
SWIMMING: The Milk Churn (NY 317 089), Easedale Tarn (NY 311 088), Codale Tarn (NY 297 088)
PLACES OF INTEREST: Heaton Cooper Studio, The Grasmere Gingerbread, Dove Cottage and The Wordsworth Museum
REFRESHMENTS: Grasmere has loads of really good cafés and pubs. They are all good so pick one you like the look of and enjoy yourself.
NEARBY SWIM SPOTS: The dubs of Far Easedale Gill offer a variety of opportunities to enjoy a swim.
OTHER FACILITIES: Toilets in the village centre, opposite the Heaton Cooper Studio and across the green on College Road. There are also toilets at Stock Lane Car Park (LA22 9SJ).

The walk up to Easedale is a treat for everyone who holds the Lake District dear, the walk being as it is, a mini-classic. The Heaton Cooper Studio ❶ is a fitting start for this walk; as his art captures the spirit of the fells here and Heaton Cooper wrote the quintessential book of Lake District tarns, *The Tarns of Lakeland*. It is a relatively easy hike with just the right amount of climbing, panoramic views and false summits to justify an extra slice of cake for lunch. Navigation is a breeze thanks to the cascading ribbon that is Sourmilk Gill; just follow it to the tarn. Whatever you do, don't miss out on the infinity pool experience at The Milk Churn ❷ on the way which is a perfect little pool hidden in plain view under the most spectacular of the falls, right next to the path.

On arrival at Easedale, you can still see the ruins of a Victorian hut, originally built to shelter ponies and their riders after their expedition to the tarn, which must have been quite exciting in long skirts and riding side saddle. According to Heaton Cooper it belonged to the commoners of Grasmere and was eventually used as a tea room, among other things, by the innkeeper of the Swan Hotel in Grasmere in what would have been the perfect place to overlook the tarn while nibbling on gingerbread and sipping tea. The innkeeper, known as 'Swanny' Wilson, even hauled a boat up to the tarn which he hired to early tarn dippers. Thanks to the backdrop of Eagle Crag and Tarn Crag as well as the dramatic moraine deposits that surround and help to form the tarn, the first view of Easedale ❸ is always a satisfying one and justifies its status as a Classic and local favourite.

Easedale is 500 metres long, around 20 metres deep and is teddy bear-shaped with two distinct basins, East (Head) and West (Body), surrounded by moraine on the eastern shore. I'm always drawn by

the solitary boulder poking through the surface on the middle of the larger of the two basins, which is often home to a pair of black-headed gulls and their nest in spring; they do a roaring trade in sandwich scraps from visiting walkers. From here swimmers can head out to the perimeter of the tarn for an interesting circumnavigation and excellent views of the surrounding fells.

The water here is crystal clear and seems to warm up quicker than most of the high tarns due to its sunny, southern aspect. The undulating bottom provides fascinating viewing thanks to the water clarity; keep an eye out for marauding shoals of colourful, stripy perch in warmer weather which provides a tropical feel unusual in a northern wild swim.

Not many people make the extra effort to visit Codale Tarn ❹ which is tucked behind Belles Knot on the steep and rocky path to the west of Easedale. This wee gem is only about 200 metres long but at 7 metres deep it is well worth the trip, and rewards the adventurous with a real tarn swimming experience; remote and hidden from the masses, it is the perfect skinny dipping location. Return back the way you came to Easedale with a satisfied spring in your step, basking in the afterglow of a cool tarn swim.

The descent route is a hop and a skip over the ford at the Easedale outflow of Sourmilk Gill (don't slip!) which takes you into the peaceful Far Easedale valley leading back towards Grasmere, with Gibson Knott and Helm Crag to keep you company along the way. Those with a botanical bent will be in their element in this valley (as will the geologists) – the wild flowers and plants light up the seeps and bogs. Keep an eye out for the insectivorous Honeydew, the Bog Pimpernel and White Beak-Sedge among others which always bring added interest and cheer to any walk.

If you fancy a treat, don't miss the turn off for Lancrigg Vegetarian Hotel for a spot of posh tea & cake, or carry on through the charming grounds of the hotel to the more down to earth Thorney How Hostel for a pint of well-kept ale by the stove. The return to Grasmere is only a kilometre away, where you can while away the remains of the day in the interesting shops, cafés and pubs of this popular Lakeland village.

## ACCOMMODATION

There is a lot of good quality hostel and B&B accommodation in Grasmere. Try Thorney How Independent Hostel situated in a 350-year-old manor only 15 minutes' walk from Grasmere village centre (015394 35597, LA22 9QW). Or if you fancy something a bit more upmarket try Lancrigg Vegetarian Country House Hotel, a country house dating from the 1600s and once occupied and renovated by poet William Wordsworth, this charming hotel with 30 acres of gardens is a lovely place to stay (015394 35317, LA22 9QN).

## WEEKEND SUGGESTION

While you are in the Vale of the Lake District Poets, you must visit Grasmere lake (as opposed to the village of Grasmere) and Rydal Water for a swim and top it off with a pint of real ale in the Badger Bar at the Glen Rothay Hotel in Rydal (015394 34500, LA22 9LR). If you are feeling adventurous, link this swim with Stickle Tarn below the Langdale Pikes and drop down into Great Langdale where you can get the number 516 bus back to Ambleside, then on to Grasmere on the number 555 (check bus times).

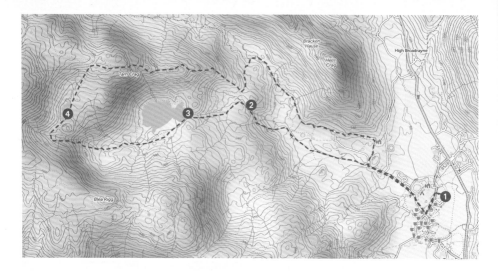

❶ From the Heaton Cooper Studio head north-east along Broadgate for about 20 meters and turn left onto Easedale Road and after about a kilometre of walking look out for the narrow footbridge that crosses Easedale Beck. Continue on the cobbled track until you come to a footpath forking off to the left which follows the course of Sourmilk Gill and continue on the valley bottom until the path begins the steady climb, following the watercourse. As the going gets steeper you will eventually come to The Milk Churn (about 2 kilometres from the footbridge over Easedale Beck); this is a very obvious fall into a perfectly proportioned pool, right by the path.
**1.9 miles**

❷ Continue north-west on up the footpath past the pools and riffles above the Churn until you hit a bit of a plateau where the path heads west and up over a couple of rises on towards the combe of Easedale Tarn. There is good path around most of the tarn and which blends into a little sheep track which follows the edge the rest of the way round. The best place to get in is the closest to the path by the outflow of Sourmilk Gill where there are some nice little shingle beaches and access to deep water, saving bare feet a punishing hobble over the rocks.
**2.5 miles**

❸ From the south-east corner of Easedale, keep to the defined path heading west leading to the northern edge of Eagle Crag looming in the distance. After a kilometre of walking and just past the steepest section of the path, adjacent to Eagle Crag and Belles Knott, a small pointed crag to the north of the path, take a lightly trodden track to the North (you may have to navigate a little here). In 300 metres you will come to Codale Tarn where you are well within your rights to shed both clothing and inhibitions before sampling some of Cumbria's finest tarn swimming.
**1 mile**

❹ From Codale Tarn head north, north-east for 500 metres, roughly following the course of the inflow gill towards the broad col above. At the col head east to pick up the path by the tarnlet heading towards Tarn Crag. From Tarn Crag the path continues to descend the ridgeline above Easedale Tarn for about a kilometre. Although the path direction fluctuates with the terrain, it essentially heads east. Just past Greathead Crag the path descends steadily in a south-easterly direction, along the final spur of the ridge, to join the path coming from Easedale Tarn. This path heads north to drop down onto the Far Easedale valley and the footbridge at Stythwaite Steps which crosses Far Easedale Gill.

Enjoy the meandering and easy-to-follow track along one of the loveliest little valleys in Lakeland, and on a nice summer day it would be madness not to take a dip in one of the many gill pools en route. As the path funnels down into a section of ravine, it opens out onto a track, passing through a small wood of conifers to the left. At the gate ahead be sure to take the detour up through the small gate to the left through the grounds of Lancrigg, and on to the track past Thorny How Hostel; it is worth a stop at one place or the other for some refreshment if you want to avoid a busy Grasmere during the summer. Follow the track back down, through the woods, onto the Easedale Road that leads over Goody Bridge and back to Grasmere Village.

**2.8 miles**

# THE VALE OF THE LAKE DISTRICT POETS

This is a classic Lake District low-level walk and it takes in the best wild swimming in the South Lakes.

## INFORMATION

DISTANCE: 6.8 miles
TIME: 6-7 hours
MAP: OS Explorer OL7 The English Lakes SE
START/END POINT: St Mary's Chapel, Rydal (NY 364 062, LA22 9LR)
PUBLIC TRANSPORT: Nearest train station is Windermere. 555 bus service between Windermere and Keswick stops metres away from the start.
PARKING: Limited parking next to St Mary's Church (honesty box on the wall) or small car park at Pelter Bridge (NY 366 059). Plenty of parking further along at White Moss Car Parks on both sides of the A591, 1.5 kilometres west of Rydal.
SWIMMING: Loughrigg Tarn (NY 347 043), Grasmere (NY 343 059), Rydal Water (NY 355 060).
PLACES OF INTEREST: Rydal Mount, Rydal Hall, Nab Cottage, Dove Cottage, Rydal Cave
REFRESHMENTS: Rydal Mount cafe (015394 33002, LA22 9LU). Badger Bar, Glen Rothay Hotel (015394 34500, LA22 9LR) - local ales, with eccentric staff and roaring fires. The Old School Room Tea Shop, Rydal Hall (015394 32050, LA22 9LX).
OTHER FACILITIES: Toilets at White Moss Car Park and the Joe the Ice Cream Man on the A591 if it's a sunny day (tell him we sent you and he'll give you free sprinkles).
ACCOMMODATION: Glen Rothay Hotel (015394 34500, LA22 9LR); Herdwick Huts (www.theherdwickhuts.co.uk); Camping at Rydal Hall (015394 32050; LA22 9LX)

*I*f you can ignore the busy road now running through the hamlet of Rydal, you can easily imagine how this scene would have appeared in the early 1800s, with only a farm track running through the vale. It still retains its old charm despite its popularity with visitors and locals alike, and it is still clear why the Lake District Poets Wordsworth, Coleridge and Southey were so inspired by the place. There are many associations with all of the Lake District Poets all around this walk, peppered as it is with astounding views and natural beauty, but it is with William Wordsworth that this part of the Lakes will be forever associated.

As an early leader of the Romantic literary movement, which celebrated nature and human emotions, William Wordsworth is regarded as one of the greatest lyric poets in the history of English literature. Wordsworth was born in Cockermouth in 1770, and went to school in Hawkshead so he knew this area well as a child. After his time at Cambridge University and following extensive walking tours in the Alps of France, Switzerland and Italy, he eventually returned to this part of Cumbria, moving to Dove Cottage in Grasmere in 1799 and then Rydal Mount in 1813. This was Wordsworth's beloved family home for the greater part of his life and he lived here for 37 years until his death in 1850 at the age of 80. He is buried nearby at St Oswald's Church in Grasmere.

It was at Rydal Mount that he wrote many of his poems, revised and improved much of his earlier works and published the final version of his most famous poem 'Daffodils' as well as the posthumous *The Prelude*, published (and named) by his widow Mary. If you have to read one epic poem in your life, as a swimmer and lover of the outdoors, I would urge you to make it *The Prelude*.

It's clearly a very personal work and shows Wordsworth as utterly in tune with nature as he was with the down-to-earth, common people – he comes across as the genuine Cumbrian that he was. He challenged what he thought of as the "gaudy and inane phraseology" of the writers of the time, choosing to phrase his writing in the language of the ordinary people; what better way to convey their simple, deeply human feelings? I find him all the more likeable, and readable, because of this.

'Daffodils' is classic Wordsworth and is as much part of the Lake District as fell walking, country sports and tea and gingerbread. Wordsworth's *Guide through the District of the Lakes* (published in 1820) also did much to encourage mass tourism to the area at a time when this was just becoming possible.

*I wandered lonely as a cloud*
*That floats on high o'er vales and hills,*
*When all at once I saw a crowd,*
*A host of golden daffodils;*
*Beside the lake, beneath the trees,*
*Fluttering and dancing in the breeze.*

*Continuous as the stars that shine*
*and twinkle on the Milky Way,*
*They stretched in never-ending line*
*along the margin of a bay:*
*Ten thousand saw I at a glance,*
*tossing their heads in sprightly dance.*

*The waves beside them danced; but they*
*Out-did the sparkling waves in glee:*
*A poet could not but be gay,*
*in such a jocund company:*
*I gazed—and gazed—but little thought*
*what wealth the show to me had brought:*
*For oft, when on my couch I lie*

*In vacant or in pensive mood,*
*They flash upon that inward eye*
*Which is the bliss of solitude;*
*And then my heart with pleasure fills,*
*And dances with the daffodils.*

William Wordsworth, *'Daffodils'*

Loughrigg Tarn ❷ is a real gem and provides the highlight of this wild swimming day. If you can hold yourself back from running down to the water's edge and diving straight in, contemplate Wordsworth's description of Loughrigg Tarn, comparing it to 'Diana's looking-glass...round, clear and bright as heaven'.

The tarn is just over 10 metres deep and about 350 metres across, ringed by a pleasant mix of alder, oak, hazel, beech and pine. The water is fringed with a wide variety of water plants including both the *Nymphaea* (white) and *Nuphar* (yellow) water lily which always add a romantic air to any wild swim. The tarn is a perfect haven for migrating wildfowl and we regularly see tufted duck, goldeneye, pochard, whooper swans and great crested grebe who seem to get along fine with the resident farm geese who are always keen to keep you company during your swim if you visit on your own.

This is a real local swimming pool, being just enough out of the way and not so easy to drive to that you can get the place to yourself most of the time. It's a nice size too; a tour of the circumference, dodging the lily beds, takes in just over 1,000 metres of swimming. Only the most narrow-minded club swimmer would resort to laps of heads-down front crawl here. This is a place for an easy breaststroke, taking in the tranquil atmosphere while pondering some

Wordsworthian verse, getting up close with the flora and fauna and admiring the views.

Grasmere ❸ follows, which gives real swimmers something to go at, although the pebbled beach next to the weir provides an ideal amphitheatre for any lakeshore activities: picnicking, paddling, fishing and certainly a swim out to 'The Island' just over half a mile away from the beach. The Victorians didn't get around to giving this island a romantic name and it is now privately owned (and access is denied), and was once used in recent times by a local farmer who rowed his sheep out there to graze every spring…I assume the grazing must be above average on the island! It always looks a very inviting island to explore and it has the enticing atmosphere of an abandoned arboretum about it, as do the smaller islands of Rydal Water ❹ and they share the same colourful smattering of Rhododendron here and there, providing a nice contrast to the deep greens of the cedar, beech and the seasonal carpet of ramsons. Swimming out to The Island is a real treat as Grasmere is a very open body of water once you make it out of the

protective mantle of the southern fells. Be warned though, when the wind whips up it can be quite daunting to be stuck out in the middle of it and you will bear the full brunt of any westerly being funnelled down the Easedale Valley, which can be lots of fun if you are used to it.

Grasmere is about a mile long, and the best swimming is to be had south of the island, the water being very shallow with a lot of silt build-up along most of the north shore; you can just make it round the island if the water level is high and the western bays are worth exploring. From the beach it is exactly 800 metres to the island if you straight-line it (and another 500 metres to circumnavigate the island if you choose to). This makes for a nice mile plus swim over some real open water where you can really open up and work up a good appetite for lunch on the beach when you return. Any section of shoreline makes for a nice swim here if you don't want to commit to going all of the way to the island, just explore the reedy bays and beaches if you'd rather, or build a fire and brew up some tea and munch Grasmere Gingerbread.

The walk along the Rothay to Rydal Water from Grasmere is a delightful one, and you soon arrive at White Moss Common for the last swim of the day. It is one of my favourite short walks in the Lakes, a favourite shared by my black lab Boot, who loves to splash through the peaty puddles and dip in the clear pools. The section of the River Rothay that flows south from White Moss is a real local secret; after the shallow pools and glides of the Rothay above, it seems impossible that any swimmable water would lie ahead. The delta that has formed there at the head of Rydal Water consists of an impenetrable looking fen of willow car, tufted sedge, alder and gigantic tussocks of purple moor-grass. In fact the river is naturally canalised here, and provides the perfect pre-amble to swimming the lake.

You have a couple of options for your swim at Rydal:

1. An out and back swim into Rydal as long as the weed beds aren't flourishing too much. This is best avoided after mid-August because of the weed growth or at any time when the river is in spate.

2. Alternatively, retrace your steps and go back over the bridge, walk around to the southern shore of Rydal Water and concentrate on swimming the deeper sections of the lake around, and to the east, of Heron Isle.

Get in at Pike Dub (keep your toes up!) and follow the Rothay downstream running the gauntlet between the surrounding fen and the lily beds and after about 300 metres you will be swimming through the bulrush and reeds that stand guard over the view of Rydal Water ahead. It is very shallow here and can be really choked with weed at the end of the summer, but it gets steadily deeper as you swim out past Swan Stone, the peninsula on your left, and on towards the small islands ahead. Be sure to look back and make a visual mark of where you came out of the reeds otherwise the return journey may prove to be a bit of a challenge. Look out for Nab Cottage, which overlooks the lake just past Swan Stone on the road side of the lake, and head on to the beguiling Isles of Rydal Water.

Who doesn't like to swim amongst islands? Heron Isle, the larger of the two, and Little Isle are perfect miniature specimens typical of the Lake District, and are worth further exploration when you get to them. The resident Canada and visiting Graylag geese often shelter in the lee of the islands and I have had some unusual swimming encounters here, including low flying geese, a rather startled otter and a grey squirrel swimming for its life from Heron Isle!

Rydal is just over a kilometre long and when you reach Heron Isle you will have covered about 700 metres. If you are in an exploratory mood you will want to continue your swim for a further 500 metres until you reach Thrang Crag, or Wordsworth's Seat situated just behind the only boathouse on the shore on the road side of the lake. It was one of William's favourite places to contemplate the world when there was only a cart track running past it.

On the walk back to St Mary's it is certainly worth taking the high road to visit Rydal Cave, which was a busy working quarry two hundred years ago, supplying the local villages with stone and which is now something of a local landmark. The view from the cave offers good views over Nab Scar and the surrounding fells and the return walk through Rydal Woods is so pretty you may even be inspired to pen a few lines of verse.

## WEEKEND SUGGESTION

Spend the weekend at the Glen Rothay Hotel, remembering to take a good second-hand book of Wordsworth's poems, and follow this walk with a jaunt up to Easedale the next day, finished off with tea and cake in Grasmere Village.

## LOUGHRIGG EXTENSION

If you are full of beans after your swim and need to burn off some energy you might fancy taking a detour to Loughrigg Fell summit (335 metres) by following the footpath just around the corner of the cottage. This contours the fell side for 400 metres before turning right at 90 degrees following a small steep gill for 500 metres which leads directly to the summit (it's a very steep 500 metres but worth the trip). Enjoy the view from the bastion that forms the summit and then head off north, north-west down the obvious path which leads first to Ewe Crag then takes a sharp westerly turn before heading down to the head of Loughrigg Terrace (this will add an extra kilometre to the walk and takes about an hour including time for 'breathers' and 'taking in the view').

**1** From St Mary's Church, walk south along the A592 for about 300 metres until you come to the little humpbacked Pelter Bridge on your right, cross the bridge and walk the Under Loughrigg Road which follows the River Rothay until you come to Fox Ghyll Country House after about 800 metres and at a very pronounced right-angled bend in the river.
**0.7 miles**

**2a** At this point you have the option of taking a shortcut, but it's a steep and gnarly one so will not be to everyone's taste. If you choose this option take the footpath that follows Fox Ghyll straight and to the right of Fox Ghyll Country House. After a kilometre of climbing, this steep path eventually leads around the edge of the high wall on your left (that you will have been following) and then left around the corner. Join the well-defined bridleway just as it starts to descend towards the stream and big stepping stones. From here you have re-joined the main route.
**0.7 miles**

**2b** If you prefer your walking to be on more predictable terrain, carry on along the Under Loughrigg Road from Fox Ghyll for another kilometre. Just before a cattle grid you will come to a steep track on the right, accessible through an open gateway and another cattle grid. Follow this steep, zig-zagging road all the way to the top of the fell, passing through a couple of gates on the way as the tarmacked

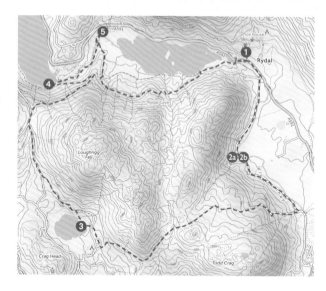

track gradually turns into an undulating rocky bridleway as you pass the last building on the fell side (which, believe it or not, used to be a golf club). This bridleway cuts the southern flank of Loughrigg Fell in half and provides a very accessible route to our favourite local tarn. Go through another gate just as the track levels off. At this point the 2a route option joins the bridleway.

Carry on following the obvious descending path, dipping down into a gully at one point to hop over the stream on the big stepping stones and remain on the obvious, broad path.

You will soon be walking around the neb of Ivy Crag, one of the many lumps and ring contours that form Loughrigg Fell (the only Lake

District fell to share its name with a tarn). Continue with the steady descent that changes direction to the north-west after Ivy Crag, proceed through the 5-bar gate until you reach a sneaky little footpath on the right running alongside a small coppice of conifers, follow this until you reach the stile and your first view of Loughrigg Tarn with the Langdale Pikes in the background.

Hop over the stile, the track and then the other stile to follow the permissive footpath across the meadow to this delightful tarn
**2.5 miles**

**3** Once changed, cut north across the meadow, hop over the rill and on to the gate which leads you back on to the track, in front of a nice old cottage.

Those with an aversion to steep hills should continue to follow the track north-west for 500 metres until you get to the small road that leads to YHA Langdale, turn right and continue up and over the brow of the hill walking on the road. Just at the crest of the hill, you will see a gate set back on the right leading to a bridleway that leads on towards the Loughrigg Terrace through the mixed woodland of Red Bank. Continue on to the Terrace until you can admire the great aerial view down to Grasmere and The Island and, on a clear day, on towards Helm Crag and Dunmail Raise in the distance. Walk all the way to the bottom, it will look as though you are going past the water's edge but carry on in one big zig, until you see the zag to the left which leads directly to the shores of Grasmere.
**1.9 miles**

④ Ignore the bridge by the weir and continue on for 700 metres until you get to Shepherd's Bridge (NY 348 063), go over the bridge towards White Moss Car Park and past the picnic benches and on to Pike Dub which lies just below the riffle in front of the picnic area and provides the unlikely start of the interesting swim into Rydal Water.
**0.6 miles**

⑤ Cross back over Shepherd's Bridge and head south up the wooded bank, take a right at the junction with the bridleway at the top (you can turn left and take the low road along the shores of Rydal if you are starting to droop and feel

the call of real ale luring you inexplicably towards the Badger Bar). Follow the wall on the right around the corner and after 100m turn left, almost back on yourself. This is the high road that rollercoasters past the edge of Jobson Close woods and takes you to Rydal Cave which can be explored (with care) once you have negotiated the huge puddle blocking the entrance via the stepping stones. There are more old quarry workings and small fissures and caves to see during the rocky descent down the track that heads off down the old spoil heap and on towards the edge of Rough

Intake Woods. Continue all the way to the shores of Rydal Water, turning right through the iron kissing gate that leads into Rydal Woods. Take any of the paths through this charming little wood and out the other side to the foot of the lake and head to your chosen tea room or drinkery for some well-earned refreshment. Take care after crossing the footbridge over the Rothay; the A591 road is very busy and the path brings you out on a blind bend. Turn right here for the return to St Mary's Chapel which is just along the road on the left.
**1.2 miles**

# WRAY CASTLE, WINDERMERE, AND THE LATTERBARROW RAMBLE

Latterbarrow is a charming summit and offers great views to the surrounding mountains and lakes and the Windermere shoreline provides ample swimming opportunities.

I t is always satisfying to include a visit to a castle on a walking route, even if it is something of a folly. Wray Castle was built in the Gothic Revival Style in 1840 along with St. Margaret's Church, by retired Liverpool surgeon, Dr James Dawson, using his wife's inheritance from a gin fortune. Apparently, she showed her contempt for it by refusing to live there, which is a shame because it has very good lake access and would have been perfect for her morning swim.

The former vicar of St Margaret's Church, Canon Hardwicke Drummond Rawnsley was related to the Dawson family and became one of the founding members of the National Trust, who now own the castle and its grounds. Canon Rawnsley became friends with Beatrix Potter when she came on holiday with her family in 1882 to visit Wray Castle. Through their friendship, he encouraged Beatrix to publish her first book, *The Tales of Peter Rabbit*. He went on to become a national figure and is remembered for his exceptional effort in preserving the special environment of the Lake District.

Over the years the castle has been a youth hostel, the home of The Freshwater Biological Association, a training college for Merchant Navy Radio officers as 'RMS Wray Castle' before eventually being opened as a visitor attraction by the National Trust.

The castle itself looks rather handsome from the outside, but there is not much to see inside, most of the rooms having been set up for the entertainment of visiting children. The café is worth a visit though and the grounds are well-maintained and are worth visiting for the sake of its specimen trees which include wellingtonia, redwood, gingko, weeping lime and beech. There is also a mulberry tree planted by William Wordsworth

## INFORMATION

DISTANCE: 5.5 miles
TIME: 4 hours
MAP: Harvey's British Mountain Map: Lake District, OS Explorer OL7 The English Lakes SE
START/END POINT: Wray Castle National Trust Car Park (NY 375 010, LA22 0JA)
PUBLIC TRANSPORT: Nearest train station is Windermere. The 505 bus runs from Kendal to Coniston, with stops at Windermere and Wray Castle Road End. Windermere Lake Cruises offer a regular Green Cruise to the boathouse at Wray between Easter and October.
SWIMMING: Red Nab (SD 385 994), High Wray Bay (NY 376 005) and Watbarrow Point (NY 377 010). Blelham Tarn (NY 367 004) is private.
PLACES OF INTEREST: Playground at Wray Castle, Wray Castle, Hawkshead Village, Grizedale Forest, Go Ape, Tarn Hows.
REFRESHMENTS: Joey's Café, Wray Castle, offers coffees and plant-based treats; Outgate Inn, Outgate (015394 68329, LA22 0NQ); good pubs and cafés in Hawkshead.
EASIER ACCESS: Direct access to Windermere from Red Nab Car Park.
NEARBY SWIM SPOTS: The shores of Windermere offer multiple opportunities to swim, Tarn Hows, High Dam, Grasmere and Rydal Water, Coniston

in 1845, a small plaque underneath it commemorates the occasion.

From the castle, the walk up to Latterbarrow follows comparatively quiet paths through the rolling countryside of Claife, passing the secluded Blelham Tarn ❷ along the way. The tarn and the bog surrounding it are a Site of Specific Scientific Interest (SSSI) as well as a Natural Nature Reserve and at the right time of year the reeds around the tarn bristle with birds and waterfowl. Access to the tarn is very tricky as it is surrounded by bog and rush and due to its SSSI status; it is not acceptable to go crashing through the rush to get to the water. If you plan to visit be respectful and do so from the gate maintained by the fishing club, who have the private fishing rights for the tarn. It is a good place to just sit and watch what flies or swims by.

Latterbarrow lies to the south of Blelham Tarn and the rambling walk to its base is easy-going and very pleasant. The steep hike to the impressive summit obelisk takes the breath away; it is a short ascent and the views are worth it. Wainwright describes Latterbarrow in his *The Outlying Fells of Lakeland* guidebook as a hill "primarily for old age pensioners and others who can no longer climb high fells". For such a diminutive hill it commands an excellent panorama of the surrounding fells and for this reason alone it is worth the hike, even for us youngsters. The last time I visited, I could see all the way to the Howgills and beyond and it was interesting to see recognisable landmarks in Ambleside in great detail.

The descent follows a winding route through the mixed woodland of Claife Heights and will especially appeal to bird and animal watchers. There is a good bird hide just off our route, overlooking Nor Moss. This is a good place to take shelter in bad weather or take a break to watch the birds

flit between the bushes. Nor Moss is part of the Claife Tarns and Mires SSSI and supports rare and declining birds typical of Atlantic oak woodland.

Finally reaching the shores of Windermere presents the opportunity to get some serious swimming in. Access to the lake is possible all the way along the lakeside track from Belle Grange ❹ to Wray Castle but the best places to get in and swim are found at Red Nab, High Wray Bay and Watbarrow Point. They all feature shingle beaches and the wide-open, exposed feeling that comes with big lake swimming. Windermere is an iconic lake among long-distance swimmers and has long been used as a training water by Channel swimming aspirants. Despite its popularity and boat traffic, it is always a thrill to swim in England's longest natural lake. This stretch of shoreline is arguably the nicest part to swim, with its regular headlands and little bays fringed with beech, oak and hazel.

The walk back to the castle passes quickly, depending on your inclination to swim, and the castle grounds are a nice place to explore after a reviving cup of coffee at the café. If you have managed to drag children around the walk they will appreciate a visit to the castle, or a play in the adventure playground situated in the woods by the car park which should tire them out nicely.

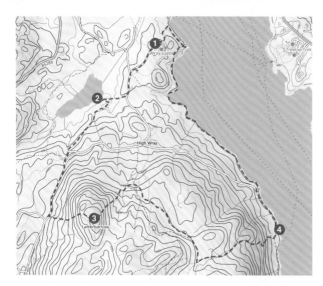

① From the car park walk around to the front of the castle and back along the entrance driveway past the hidden tower of St Margaret's Church, to the gatehouse. Turn left at the road and follow the footpath on the side of the road which threads through trees for about 200 metres where an unmarked footpath leads west towards Blelham Tarn, which is hidden in the trees ahead. Continue on the path and over a little stone bridge which leads to a kissing gate at the edge of a copse, follow the path through the copse to another gate leading out into the meadow ahead. Turn right here to get a fleeting glimpse of the lovely but private Blelham Tarn, and head north down to a gate in the fence which leads to a boathouse and a good view of the tarn.
**0.6 miles**

② Retrace your steps to the gate by the copse and continue on the south side of the meadow. Yellow arrow footpath markers point the way to a stile where the wall meets the fence. Head south along the edge of the field to another stile by the beck. Continue on the grassy track over pastureland heading south-west, carry on through the gate and on to Hole House farm buildings. Pass through the gate and farm to the road and turn right, heading south, south-west. The road filters onto another road after about 150 metres, turn right onto this road and keep walking south, south-west.

Pass the copse bordered with hazel on the left, the road passes over a small beck by another stand of trees and soon comes to a footpath on the left, signposted Latterbarrow. Go through the gate and follow the steep path due east, to the woods ahead where the path forks. Take the left fork which heads east and follow the well-worn path to the impressive stone monument on the summit.
**1.2 miles**

③ Head off the summit following the north, north-easterly path in the direction of Windermere and the distant, but distinct outline of Ill Bell in the distance. Head through the small gate in the wall, following the right of way downhill and through the trees that leads towards Waterson Intake. Cross the gill where the retaining fence meets the wall and continue north-east through the woods. Go over the stile in the fence which leads immediately onto a forest track, carry on left following the sweeping bend down to a forest gate and turn right towards the National Trust Basecamp site (don't enter).

Go through the gate and take the footpath that runs south-east alongside the wall of Basecamp which is signed Nor Moss, Near Sawrey. Stay on the forest track for about 300 metres when the track crosses a deer gate, continue on the single track through the conifers still heading south-east. The track broadens and winds through the trees before reaching another deer gate. Go through the gate, 50 metres to the left is a bird hide, which overlooks Nor Moss (but is sadly obscured by bushes).

Retrace your steps to the deer gate and carry on the track following the wall, heading south-east. The track soon merges with the forest road, stay left and follow the road to the crossroads. Take the left-hand bridleway signed Belle Grange heading due east. Descend on this good footpath as it blends into a cobbled track which leads to Belle Grange and the Windermere shoreline.
**1.7 miles**

4 Turn right at the shoreline path to take a short detour south to visit the Bark Barn and the jetty at Bass Rock which gives a great view of Windermere. Return to the shoreline path and head north, past Belle Grange and on towards Red Nab. Stay on the track for 2 kilometres, past Red Nab car park and on past a couple of boathouses to High Wray Bay where there is a gate in the wall on the right leading to Wray Castle Estate. Follow the shore path past the handsome stone boathouse where there is a nice gravel beach which is the perfect entry place for swimming the bay.

Stay on the shoreline path and continue around the bay. Just before the steps that lead up towards the wood and the castle (now in view) there is another nice gravel beach which is good for swimming in the shelter of the oak and hazel. Carry on up the steps turning right at the top and head north-east towards the woods. Go through the iron gate in the fence and follow the woodland path down towards Watbarrow Point, a good place to view the boats on the lake going to and fro. Continue on the woodland path that now shadows Low Wray Bay to the black boathouse with the corrugated roof and turn left at the iron fence which is signposted for the Castle Main Entrance. Soon the car park hovers into view, beneath the castle.
**2 miles**

*Walk 19*

# STAVELEY, THE RIVER KENT AND THE TARNS OF POTTER FELL

Fuelled by the cafes of Mill Yard, Staveley is perfectly situated to launch an adventure, with Potter Tarn, Gurnal Dubs and the River Kent within striking distance.

## INFORMATION

**DISTANCE:** 6.1 miles
**TIME:** 4 hours
**MAP:** Harvey's British Mountain Map: Lake District, OS Explorer OL7 The English Lakes SE
**START/END POINT:** St Margaret's Tower (SD 472 981, LA8 9LN)
**PUBLIC TRANSPORT:** Staveley has its own train station with a regular service. Served by the number 555 bus which runs from Lancaster to Keswick stopping in Staveley.
**SWIMMING:** Potter Tarn (SD 494 988), Gurnal Dubs (SD 501 991), River Kent (SD 488 979)
**PLACES OF INTEREST:** The Mill Yard (shops, cafés and pub), St Margaret's Tower, St James Church, Lakeland Farm Visitor Centre, Windemere Canoe Kayak
**REFRESHMENTS:** Wilf's Café, Staveley (01539 822329, LA8 9LR); The Eagle and Child, Staveley (01539 821320, LA8 9LP)
**EASIER ACCESS:** Good access to Windermere from Bowness.
**NEARBY SWIM SPOTS:** Windermere

Staveley and the fells that surround it are overlooked by the majority of visitors to the Lake District. Although the terrain here is much less dramatic than the heart of the Lakes, it provides good access to Kentmere for mountain biking, hill walking and swimming, and to Potter Fell, which contains some real swimming gems. The River Kent passes through the village and is a good trout stream and contains some small but diverting pools worthy of note. Staveley has an energetic population of mainly outdoor sport-loving locals, and it has its own amiable and down-to-earth atmosphere. There are two social hubs: The Eagle and Child pub and the Mill Yard, which contains the legendary Wilf's Café, a very large bike shop and the more recent addition of the Hawkshead Brewery. All in all, if you want to get away from the hotspots of the Lakes it provides quite a nice change.

The walking along this route is a nice change too. Although it has its steep spots, there are none of the relentless ascents of the central fells, yet the walking remains stimulating and enjoyable throughout. Our route joins the Dales Way at the River Kent along what must be one of the prettiest stretches of the river.

St Margaret's Tower provides the starting point for this walk ❶. St Margaret's has stood for nearly 700 years and was founded in 1338 and is not in a bad state considering. It was built by Sir William de Thweng, Lord of Staveley, and was an important part of the community for hundreds of years, providing spiritual sustenance to the village, along with education as its dual-use was as a meeting place and school up until the early 19th century. The amble up to the surrounding lowland fells and tarns from

Staveley takes a pleasant route through a very pastoral scene.

The first of the tarns is Potter Tarn ❷, a nice place to swim if a little bleak in appearance. It features an outsize dam wall with serious buttressing on the dry side and is a good place to cool off after the ascent from the village. The tarn was used to supply water to the Croppers Paper Mill in Burneside as its nearest tarn neighbour does to this day. Unfortunately however, poor old Potter Tarn will always be overshadowed by its more attractive neighbour Gurnal Dubbs ❸, which lies a kilometre to the west.

The unusual name can be traced back to the ownership of the tarn. Gurnal is a local family name dating from the 16th century, and a dub is of course, a dialect word meaning 'pool'. Gurnal Dubs would mean the pools belonging to the Gurnal Family (Gambles, 1980). Gurnal Dubs used to be three separate tarns (hence the plural, dubs) but the construction of the dam merged the three together into one larger tarn. The tarn supplies water to Croppers along the valley in Burneside, its flow being controlled by the concrete dam. The dam wall has been very tastefully done and together with the boathouse at its western end, creates a kind of 'lido in the fells' ambience. The boathouse was built for the Fothergill family of Lowbridge House which has since been renovated and is in a very good condition.

The water level of the tarn is much lower than it used to be as the dam was lowered in 1990, but as it stands it is just about as perfect as you can get for relaxed outdoor swimming. On a hot summer's day, you could be forgiven for spending the rest of the day here, but there is more water to seek out and some quiet river pools to discover, so rouse yourself and sally on!

The rapid descent back down Potter Fell takes you past the tempting but well-fenced-off Ghyll Pool ❹ and straight down to the Dales Way which runs along the River Kent ❺ all the way back to the Staveley road. Along the way are some lovely paddling pools and a great swimmable glide near Beckmickle Ing. The walk back to Staveley from here on is all on level paths, running alongside the river through meadows and woodland and is nothing short of idyllic. The return to the village is all the better for visiting The Eagle and Child or Wilf's Café and is the best way to round off such a satisfying day out.

❶ Take the footpath to the left of the ruins of St. Margaret's Tower, carry on through the walled walkway and over the bridge which crosses the River Kent. Turn right once over the bridge and follow the footpath for about 50 metres where the path forks, take the left fork up the bank heading east, north-east, until you get to the road. Continue on the road for 200m, taking the left-hand fork. Stay on the road up the steep zig-zag that passes Craggy Plantation on the left (a nice,

wooded walk in itself). Once past the plantation and over the cattle grid, stay on the road for another 300 metres as it continues to climb, keeping an eye out for the right of way on the right. This takes the form of a farm track leading off to the right in a north-easterly direction and is signposted.
**0.9 miles**

❷ Take the farm track, go through the gate then on through another gate then stay on the track until you reach the buildings at Frost Hole.

Once at the cottages, go down the ginnel between the buildings, through the gate and turn immediately left which takes you past a charming garden and on to a walled and wooded path heading north, north-east. Go through the gate at the end of this short pathway and on to the open fellside. Once through the gate follow the sign pointing right, marked 'Potter's Path'. It heads steeply up onto the fellside, heading roughly east, south-easterly, through a couple of gates and eventually descends gently down towards Potter Tarn, which really stands out with its outsized dam wall.

Break away from the path to head to the tarn for a swim. This is a lovely place for a swim and a cool off after the steep walking.
**1 mile**

❸ Head back onto the path that leads to a stone stile in the wall above the near shore of the tarn. Drop down in front of the imposing dam wall and take the north-east path up to the wall on the other side of the dam and hop over the stone stile to get onto the path that leads directly to Gurnal Dubs. This takes you on a pleasant ascent over open fellside, through another wall and onwards to crest the top after about 600 metres where you will be greeted with the wonderful sight of Gurnal Dubs. Here is a place to linger, take in the views, walk around the tarn and enjoy a long swim in a truly wonderful setting.
**1.2 miles**

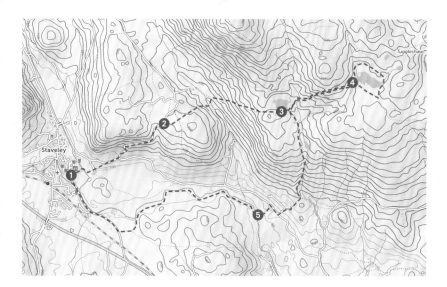

❹ After your swim, retrace your steps to the dam wall of Potter Tarn to begin the descent back down to the River Kent. At the dam wall, turn your back to the wall and head south following the little gill that emanates from the tarn, down the grassy track that leads through multiple gates and passes the inviting but forbidden Ghyll Pool. Keep on the path all the way down the fell to a deciduous spinney. Just before the end of the spinney, the path forks by an iron gate, take the footpath to the right. The path here is very overgrown but eventually leads to the farm at Hundhowe with its wonderful old buildings. Keep going past the farm buildings until you reach the road, then turn right heading north-west.

Walk along the road for no more than 150 metres until you are just past all of the buildings at Hagg Foot Farm. Take the unmarked gate which is found right up against the wall of the last building. This takes you around the back of the Hagg Foot buildings and leads past a paddock area, fuel tank and greenhouse on a hard road, and on to a track that bears to the right and takes you down to Hagg Foot Bridge.
**1.5 miles**

❺ Take the bridge over the River Kent and once over the bridge turn right and follow the small path that follows the river upstream. The path here is part of the Dales Way and provides a lovely bit of walking. Keep on the path, through the mighty gate stones of the huge old barn that towers above, and onwards towards Beckmickle Ing. Undulating along the course of the river, this path will take you all the way back to the road that leads into Staveley, through gates and over stiles, just stick with it and enjoy the walking. There is some good dipping to be had along the banks of the Kent here too. Keep an eye out for the deep glide, which is a favourite of the author; it is situated just down the bank from a prominent oak and a very productive crab apple tree.

The path eventually funnels the walker into a wall-lined path, which leads away from the river and on towards the main road. Turn right at the road and follow it back into Staveley until you see the welcome sign of The Eagle and Child, carry on a 100 meters or so down the road to St Margaret's Tower and the end of the walk.
**1.5 miles**

# Walk 20

# WINDERMERE, MOSS ECCLES AND WISE EEN TARN

This walk not only leads you to one of Beatrix Potter's favourite tarns, but it also passes one of the best pubs in the Lakes.

*N*ear and Far Sawrey are tucked away behind Claife Heights and enjoy an altogether more pastoral way of life compared to the hustle and bustle of the Lake District honey pots. Merely being in Far Sawrey seems to lower the blood pressure and although the sylvan Claife Heights lacks the drama of the high mountains, it more than makes up for it with its intimate beauty and charm. No doubt this fact wasn't lost on Beatrix Potter, the most famous resident of the village of Near Sawrey. Her 17th-century Hill Top farmhouse is lovingly maintained by the National Trust, to whom she left it, and is very much worth a visit outside of the busy summer season. Potter also owned Moss Eccles Tarn which served as an inspiration for some of her children's stories.

For the swim hiker Sawrey is a blessing, routes from the village connect the all-encompassing shoreline of Windermere with some of the most delightful tarns in the region along the way. The walk over the Heights to Windermere provides a good start to the walking as it pushes gently up through pastureland before dropping through the woods to the lake. The path joins the lakeshore just opposite some of Windermere's most handsome islands, the Lilies of the Valley (named for the rare flower that once flourished there) and Thompson's Holme. The islands are fun to visit from the water but take great care in crossing to them and wear a tow float if you do. The Windermere ferries tear through here at a fair rate of knots – you have been warned!

All along the lake shoreline can be found the multi-stemmed trees of hazel, oak and ash indicative of traditional coppicing

## INFORMATION

DISTANCE: 6.1 miles
TIME: 5 hours
MAP: Harvey's British Mountain Map: Lake District, OS Explorer OL7 The English Lakes SE
START/END POINT: Braithwaite Hall, Far Sawrey (SD 378 953, LA22 0LQ)
PUBLIC TRANSPORT: Nearest train station is Windermere. Car/passenger ferry runs from Ferry Nab, Bowness to Ferry House, not far from Far Sawrey. The 505 bus connects Windermere with Hawkshead via Ambleside. Mountain Goat offers the 525 seasonal shuttle service from Hawkshead to Sawrey. Taxi is the simplest and cheapest option.
SWIMMING: Bass Rock, Windermere (SD 388 988), Wise Een Tarn (SD 370 975), Moss Eccles Tarn (SD 372 968)
PLACES OF INTEREST: Hill Top, Claife Viewing Station, Hawkshead Village, Grizedale Forest, Go Ape, Tarn Hows
REFRESHMENTS: Tower Bank Arms, Near Sawrey (015394 36334, LA22 0LF); Cuckoo Brow Inn, Far Sawrey (015394 43425, LA22 0LQ); Boathouse Café at Esthwaite Water Trout Fishery (015394 36541, LA22 0QF). Good pubs and cafés in Hawkshead.
EASIER ACCESS: Direct access to Windermere from Red Nab Car Park and at Ferry House.
NEARBY SWIM SPOTS: Windermere shoreline offers multiple opportunities to swim, Tarn Hows, High Dam, Grasmere and Rydal Water, Coniston

methods. By the mid-17th century most of the trees in this area had been felled to feed the local iron industry which had been expanding for hundreds of years. The charcoal burn platforms are still visible as circular level sites, but thankfully by the end of the 18th century, the woodland was replanted and well managed, growing into the dense canopy and diverse woodland that we can enjoy today.

The shoreline is home to our only native balsam, Touch Me Not Balsam, whose delicate yellow flowers bloom from July to September. The very rare Netted Carpet Moth feeds exclusively on Touch Me Not Balsam and this is one of the few places in Britain that this moth calls home. Lepidopterists stay alert!

Bass Rock ❸, at the end of our section of shoreline path, is a significant landmark for swimmers. When swimming a one-way length of Windermere it marks the beginning of the last straight into Waterhead and is a very welcome sight. It is a good place to access the water for a swim too and is also the site of the Bark Barn and a nice new jetty, where a ferry from Brockhole visits as part of its seasonal lake crossing service. The Bark Barn was built in the 18th century to store bark from coppiced oak to supply the local tanneries.

The hike up alongside Belle Grange Beck from Bass Rock enters the Claife Tarns and Mires Site of Specific Scientific Interest (SSSI) near Scab Moss. The site includes all of the 'mosses' and tarns and is a haven for aquatic and wetland plants and damsel and dragonflies. Scab Moss itself is a nationally rare habitat and sustains a number of specialist species such as the Black Darter, Britain's smallest dragonfly and the downy emerald dragonfly with its bright green eyes. Insectivorous plants also thrive here including sundew and lesser bladderwort (whose underwater bladders suck in unsuspecting insects) and the lovely Parnassus, or Bog Star which flowers in the autumn.

Maintaining the bogs on Claife has an important role to play and not just for the biodiversity they offer. Protecting the peat reduces carbon emissions helping to mitigate climate change as well as reducing soil runoff into Windermere and providing essential wildlife corridors.

Reaching the tarns after the climb up from Windermere brings a welcome return to swimming opportunities. Wise Een Tarn ❹ is tucked away behind a spinney of larch and is surrounded by marshy ground containing Devil's Bit Scabious, Bittercress, Water Mint, Sundew, Sphagnum and Rush. It is best to head for the dry ground in the woods to get changed for swimming and in the summer months you may have to push through the excessive lily growth to get to the clear water by the boathouse. It is a nice place to swim, if a little peaty and I've never met another swimmer here.

As noted by Heaton-Cooper in *The Tarns of Lakeland*, the tarns are all man-made by the damming of the marshland and they have been stocked with fish by the Freshwater Biological Association for research. The track between Wise Een with Moss Eccles Tarn is an ancient right of way and cart track linking Sawrey with Colthouse at the head of Esthwaite Water. It provides a nice path for the ramble down to Moss Eccles which materialises in the near distance during the descent.

Moss Eccles Tarn ❺ was bought by Beatrix Potter in 1926, 13 years after she married local solicitor William Heelis. She planted the water lilies there and stocked it with trout, and she left it to the National Trust who are its current owners. The tarn was a favourite place for them to spend time together in the evenings where Potter enjoyed drawing while Heelis fished. They kept a boat here to row about the tarn which was recovered from the tarn in the 1970s and is now housed in the Windermere Steamboat Museum. It is thought that Moss Eccles Tarn, along with Esthwaite Water, provided the inspiration for *The Tale of Mr. Jeremy Fisher*, one of Potter's much-loved children's books.

As a place for swimming and general lounging about on a sunny day, Moss Eccles is hard to beat. The rocky outcrops at the dam end to the south hold the heat of the sun and dry out wet towels and clothes a treat. The tarn itself can be rather murky when the peaty bottom is disturbed (it makes lovely tea!) although this doesn't detract from the pleasure of swimming here and a tour of the lily fringes is a real treat.

Near Sawrey is quickly reached from Moss Eccles, following the old track which also provides an alternative shortcut straight back to Far Sawrey if necessary. It would be a shame to miss out on Near Sawrey though, it is a picture-perfect village and there are often little honesty stalls to be found outside the cottages, offering perfect homemade scones and cakes worth far more than the suggested price. This is also the location of Hill Top and the Tower Bank Arms, which both warrant a visit. The Tower Bank Arms is a genuine Lake District pub, one of the best in the district and its welcoming open doors and warm interior should not be forsaken following a day of chilly swimming and vigorous hiking. It provides an ideal end to the day before the easy walk across the meadow to return to Brathwaite Hall and the journey home.

❶ From Braithwaite Hall car park, walk directly over the road to the start of the footpaths signposted there (next to the phone box defibrillator), take the left-hand path that will lead you up onto Claife Heights, heading north. After 300 metres the track forks, keep on the right-hand track, bordered by a stone wall to the left and pastureland to the right. The track leads to a gate, closely followed by a track crossroads. Continue straight on, heading roughly north-east, following the signpost towards Windermere Lakeshore.

This footpath now takes you down through Harrow Slack leading towards the Windermere shoreline. The track gives way to perfect single track and if you have had an early start, you may be rewarded with the sight of beams of sunlight streaming through the mixed woodland straight towards you from the east. Stay on the path, ignoring the many side tracks, until the path is heading directly north when you will soon join the main track that runs along the lakeshore.
**1.4 miles**

❷ The shoreline here has many mini bays and gravel beaches which lend themselves to swimming. 2 kilometres on from joining the main track, the imposing mass of the Bark Barn will hover into view on the right of the track. This marks the location of Bass Rock.
**1.1 miles**

❸ Just north of the Bark Barn, take the signposted track left, up the cobbled path towards Hawkshead. The path zig-zags up above Belle Grange and forks after about 400 metres. Take the right fork which continues to ascend, a little less steeply on towards two more forks in the path – stay right on both counts as you pass a column of Scots Pine just as the terrain levels out and becomes more open, amongst a plantation of young pine.

At Scab Moss, there is a slightly confusing crossroads but stick with the direction of the signpost pointing in the direction of 'Sawrey, via Tarns' and take the smaller path across the crossroads and to the left, heading south-west, which will bring you back to the head of Belle Grand Beck (ignore the path to the right pointing towards 'Hawkshead via Guide Posts'). Stay on the path for 500 metres, staying left at the fork in the path just after crossing the beck.

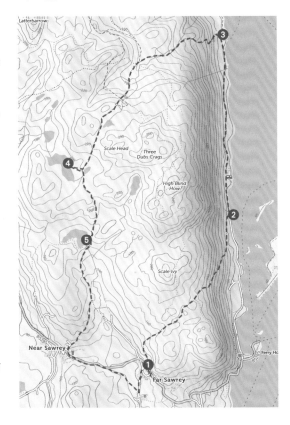

The next crossroads is very straightforward, continue straight ahead and stay on this path which continues through the woods and soon joins the forest road and passes Highs Moss, a very overgrown and moss-ridden tarn, positively stuffed with wildlife, on the left. Here the terrain opens up again and continues to do so as the boundary wall of Scale Head comes into view and the road deteriorates into rough track. Pass through the gate in the wall and stay on the south, south-westerly track as it descends gently down the open fell where you will see the glimmer of Wise Een Tarn ahead and to the right.

Wise Een is best accessed by walking down to the small, dammed tarn right next to the

path and then making a beeline west, over rough ground towards the tarn. Depending on the time of year, and level of lily growth in the tarn, the most accessible swimming entry point is at the north-eastern corner.
**1.5 miles**

**4** After exploring Wise Een Tarn, head back to the main track by the dammed tarn and continue heading south, through the gate, gradually ascending, until the track leaves the wall and begins the gentle slope down towards Moss Eccles Tarn.
**0.6 miles**

**5** From the tarn, continue due south on the track, through the gate and begin the descent to Near Sawrey. The track forks at

the farm buildings, stay right to continue down to Near Sawrey (taking the left fork leads directly back to Far Sawrey and provides a convenient short cut if needed). At Near Sawrey, turn left heading towards the excellent Tower Bank Arms and past Hill Top and pick up the footpath just over the wall from the road and on the same side as Hill Top. This is a good little path, and it follows the road for about 500 metres before heading south-east across the meadows to Town End and St Peter's Church at Far Sawrey. Turn left onto the road at Town End and follow it north for 250 metres to the main road then turn right to return to Braithwaite Hall.
**1.5 miles**

# FINSTHWAITE, HIGH DAM AND THE RIVER LEVEN

Finsthwaite and the surrounding countryside is delightful and High Dam is a real local's swimming pool which gives a lot for a relatively short walk in.

*F*insthwaite village ❷ is a world away from the busy centres of Windermere, Ambleside and Keswick. Life moves at a different pace here and the visitor can experience, in some way, what life must have been like in Cumberland a century ago. My good college friend Claire lived in Finsthwaite, and I stayed with her once during the summer holidays. We were roped in by the farmer to help bring in and pile up bales of hay from the meadows that surround the village, which was hard, hot work in the blazing summer sun. Sitting on the bales after all of the hard work was done, watching the sun go down over Finsthwaite Heights drinking a cold beer remains one of my happiest memories.

You can get to the start of this walk using the Lakeside and Haverthwaite Railway. It is always a treat to arrive by steam train and the quirky little café at Haverthwaite Station is exceptional. Nevertheless, the car park at Lakeside is vast and is a better option if you plan to cross over using the ferry, and swim in the river.

The walk up to High Dam ❸ passes through Great Knott Wood, leads up through Finsthwaite village and on to High Dam passing through the woods that supplied Stott Park Bobbin Mill ❹ with wood for its bobbins. Walking through ancient woodland sites like this is a great pleasure and it is lovely to see how the Woodland Trust are managing the woods at Great Knott. The Trust is restoring the native broadleaf tree habitat using the traditional method of 'snigging' to thin out the non-native conifers: this involves using logging teams of Belgian Ardennes horses who drag out the conifers, scarifying the ground and leaving it in an ideal state to regenerate with native broadleaved trees. The woods

## INFORMATION

**DISTANCE:** 4.1 miles
**TIME:** 3 hours
**MAP:** Harvey Maps: Lake District BMC (British Mountain Maps), OS Explorer OL7 The English Lakes SE
**START/END POINT:** Lakeside Car Park (SD 378 873, LA12 8AT)
**PUBLIC TRANSPORT:** Nearest train station is Oxenholme. Then take a taxi to Lakeside.
**SWIMMING:** High Dam Tarn (SD 362 887), Low Dam Tarn (SD 364 8836), River Leven at Fell Foot (SD 380 870)
**PLACES OF INTEREST:** Stott Park Bobbin Mill, Fell Foot Park, The Lakeside and Haverthwaite Railway, Lakeland Motor Museum
**REFRESHMENTS:** Lakeside Hotel, Lakeside (015395 30001, LA12 8AT); Oscar's Café Lakeside Station Building, Lakeside (015395 30153, LA12 8AS); The Station Tea Room at Haverthwaite Station is excellent (015395 31594, LA12 8AL)
**EASIER ACCESS:** Level access to Windermere from Fell Foot Park.
**NEARBY SWIM SPOTS:** The Tarns and River Kent at Staveley, Millerground Public Jetties on Windermere.

here are also home to the red squirrel and a wealth of native flora.

The area has a fascinating industrial history. From the 12th century, charcoal burning and leather tanning were carried out in the woods, but it is the bobbin mill that this area is most associated with. In the 19th century, the Yorkshire and Lancashire cotton trade brought a huge demand for wooden bobbins which were supplied by the Stott Park Bobbin Mil. Opened in 1835, the mill was perfectly situated due to the abundance of natural resources that surround it to this day – water to power the mill and coppiced woodland for the bobbins. It was one of the few mills to have been specifically built to manufacture bobbins and flourished due to its proximity to the railway line, giving it a distinct advantage over other mills at the time. High Dam was built by the mill owners to help provide water power to the mill before the site was converted to use electricity in 1941. We swimmers have a lot to thank them for, along with the Lake District Special Planning Board. They purchased it in 1973 to allow public access to the tarn, allowing open access to the water and woods surrounding it.

An old cart track leads up from the north of Finsthwaite and follows the beck that flows from the dams above. The woods of oak and birch give way to larch and mature Scots pine along the way

and the woodland floor is cushioned with bracken and bilberry. As the steep track levels out, the first of the dammed tarns comes into view: Low Dam. Although it is a mere shadow of High Dam it is a fine place for a swim and is a little like a swimming pool in that has a shallow and a deep end, perfect for children or beginners.

Cresting the well-constructed wall of local stone and looking out across the waters of High Dam for the first time the swimmer is filled with a sense of well-being. This is a place we can call home for a while and the intimacy of the heather, dangling larch and old pine add to that feeling. Many a happy hour can be spent here, lazily swimming about the lily pads gazing between the trees to the distant hazy fells.

The return walk through the woods to the east of the tarn is very rewarding, the ancient walls and tracks are softened with great pillows of moss and lead to the gates of the bobbin mill, which is very much worth a visit.

Back at the spacious car park at Lakeside there is swimming to be had if you have the time. Windermere Lake Cruises, in conjunction with the National Trust normally run a shuttle ferry over to Fell Foot Park ❹ directly opposite between 10:00-16:00 during the summer season. This gives ideal access to the River Leven which offers some fantastic river swimming all the way down to the Swan Hotel and back, a round trip of just over 2 kilometres. The distance isn't great, but gentle swimmers beware, it can take three times as long to get back up the river than the swim downstream! You must master the noble art of eddy hopping to make it back against the flow. **Please note:** The ferry service to Fell Foot has been temporarily suspended until Covid restrictions end at Fell Foot at the time of writing but should resume in the very near future.

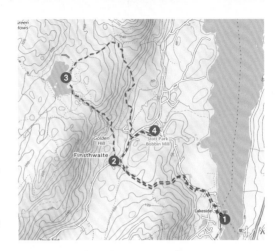

**1** Head out of the car park and turn right on to the road heading north. Take care on this road, it can get dangerously busy. Follow the signs for 'Great Knott Wood Walk' along the road. After about 200 metres turn off the road and into Knott Wood and continue to follow the green arrows that take you along the wooded path which offers a safe alternative to the road, and which follows its course. This soon leads to a wall, which borders the signposted footpath up into the woods. The broad gravel track eventually forks – take the right fork, then a little further on take the right fork again.

As you come to the edge of the woods, hop over the gated stile, and walk across the meadow towards St Peter's Church in Finsthwaite. Pass through the gate at the end of the meadow path and on to a paved path that takes you past the church. The road forks here, take the left fork towards the small post box visible on the main village road.
**0.9 miles**

**2** Turn right at the road, then left after a few meters, following the footpath signposted for 'High Dam ½ mile'. Walk across the nice gravel driveway and on up the thin path ahead to another little gated stile and cross the meadow heading north. Go through the gate in the wall by some caravans, ignore the farm track to the left, take the right-hand path still heading north following the yellow footpath arrows. Pass the crab

apple trees in the meadow and go through the gate and over the bridge into the woods. Pick up the main cart track that cuts uphill through the woods heading north-west. Stay on the main track which ascends steadily beside the gill which runs down to the bobbin mill. At the fork in the track next to a prominent larch stay left still heading north-west.

Follow the yellow Greenwood Trails sign ignoring the inviting looking path over the bridge to the left and keep ascending on the broad track. Soon the small tarn at Low Dam will come into view. In summer this pool is a good spot to cool off after the climb and gives a taste of what is to come. To get to High Dam, rejoin the path and carry on over the small bridges and up to the main dam wall which is less than 50 metres up from Low Dam.
**0.6 miles**

**3** After exploring and swimming High Dam, rejoin the footpath that follows the eastern shore and follow it north-east, taking the right fork in the path, heading straight for the boundary wall and through the kissing gate. Follow the east, north-easterly path through the bracken crossing the open fellside, eventually following the deer fence to the right. Keep going straight on at the gated area, remaining on the descending track. By an old rowan tree take the footpath forking right (easily missed), heading east off the main track through the bracken just as it begins to level out.

At the next gate turn right through the woods, which are predominantly silver birch. Carry on along the cobbled path and through the old stone gateway. Follow the ancient, moss-walled path heading roughly south, south-east. At a distinct bend in

the walled path, follow the path marked by a stone step and yellow footpath arrow, which leads south-west following a short fence, then on to a wall on the left. Follow the lovely winding path through the oak and birch to a gap in the wall. Take the path left just after the gap in the wall, down through the woods turning left at the fork which leads to a wall and lots of brambles. This path comes out onto the road near the Finsthwaite car park (used for High Dam). Go through the car park to the Finsthwaite road and turn left and follow the roadside path, taking the next right turn towards Stott Park Bobbin Mill and explore.
**1.4 miles**

④ From the bobbin mill, retrace your steps, passing the Finsthwaite car park and head towards the village. Turn left at the first building which is Church View Cottage and carry on to St Peter's Church to return to the Lakeside via the approach route.

Once back at Lakeside, if there is time and if the ferry to Fell Foot is running, do take the opportunity to have a swim in the River Leven, it is worth it. From the ferry pier, head into the main park following the shore of what is at this point, the beginning of the Leven. The best place to get in and swim is at the stone slipway. Just look out for boat

traffic and remember that the flow downstream can be quite strong, especially after heavy rain. Remember when swimming upstream, avoid the main flow in the centre of the river and stay in the slack water and eddies close to the riverbanks. Just round the corner from the park, there is a nice slow-moving bend, fringed with water lilies. If you can't make it back upstream just get out on the eastern bank and walk back.
**1.2 miles**

# SCOAT TARN AND LOW TARN

The walk into this mountain bowl containing the gems of Scoat Tarn and Low Tarn is wild and remote and offers spectacular swimming.

## INFORMATION

**DISTANCE:** 6.2 miles
**TIME:** 5 hours
**MAP:** Harvey's British Mountain Map: Lake District,OS Explorer OL6 The English Lakes SW
**START/END POINT:** Overbeck Bridge Car Park (NY 168 068)
**PUBLIC TRANSPORT:** The nearest train station is Seascale, near Gosforth. Take a taxi from there.
**SWIMMING:** Nether Beck (NY 159 074), Scoat Tarn (NY 158 103), Low Tarn (NY 161 093)
**PLACES OF INTEREST:** Wasdale Head, Hardknott Castle Roman Fort, Ravenglass and Eskdale Railway
**REFRESHMENTS:** The Sawmill Cafe & Farm Shop, Nether Wasdale (019467 26716, CA20 1ET); Wasdale Head Inn, Wasdale Head (019467 26229, CA20 1EX)
**EASIER ACCESS:** Reasonable access on the north-western shore of Wast Water.
**NEARBY SWIM SPOTS:** Wast Water, Eskdale, Burnmoor Tarn, Styhead, Sprinkling Tarn

There is something wild about the fells surrounding Mosedale that sets them apart from the more popular areas of Lakeland. The feeling of euphoric detachment that comes from being alone in the mountains over time is achieved sooner and is stronger here than in any other place I know of. This route follows Nether Beck into the combes of Scoat Fell and Red Pike and takes the path less travelled. A good understanding of the basics of navigation and how the ground relates to the contours of the map is essential here in poor weather.

The swimmer's interest is piqued within the first few miles walking up Nether Beck, where the rushing water beckons anyone with even the slightest sense of adventure. The deep gorges of the beck are present right from the outset and hold bewitching, dark pools with rushing falls of white water at their heads. The great curve of the valley path to the tarns links a series of hanging valleys which transport the wanderer deeper and deeper into fascinating terrain, the ever-present rushing beck leading the way to the ultimate goal above.

Lying below Scoat Fell and Red Pike are the glacial bowls which hold Scoat Tarn ❸ and Low Tarn ❹. These are some of the highest tarns in the region and look out over the fells beyond Yewbarrow and Wast Water and on towards Burnmoor Tarn and the Scafells.

Scoat Tarn hides from view until the very last minute and reveals itself as the boggy path crests its basin. It has an open aspect despite the crags above which is unusual for such a deep corrie tarn. Everywhere about the tarn are huge boulders scattered haphazardly by the might of retreating glaciers, distorting the sense of scale, and adding to the drama of the place. On a calm day the silence of the

tarn is astonishing, with just the faintest murmur of the outflow audible. The water is sweet and clear, with rocky margins and waving clumps of weed giving way to a black peat base as the water deepens. Swimming in Scoat Tarn is the embodiment of mountain swimming. It is swimming for the sheer sensuality of the experience and is enhanced by solitude and humility.

The ground around the tarn is thick with peat and the walk over to Low Tarn across one of the spurs of Red Pike is springy with Beak Sedge, Bog Asphodel, Bell Heather and Sphagnum. From the spur the full aspect of the fells to the east can be appreciated, but what draws the eye is Low Tarn in the shallow combe below, with its tiny satellite tarns glinting in the light. It lacks the dramatic surroundings of Scoat Tarn, but Low Tarn certainly has its own charm, and the water is clear and dark with the peat of its base. It is hard to leave such a place, but the descent is something to look forward to and follows the wonderfully named Brimfull Beck before heading off over High Fell and on to the broad spur of Knott Ends. The walking is easy on the legs until the steep drop down to Over Beck with its green-blue pebble pools, and the car park is soon reached via the valley path.

**1** From the car park, turn right onto the road and continue over the bridge past Bowderdale Farm, over Nether Beck Bridge crossing the cattle grid until the bridleway on the right sign posted for Haycock is reached after about a kilometre of walking.

The steep path soon levels out and offers a nice walk into the valley with impressive views of Yewbarrow and Wast Water to the east. About a kilometre from the road, the falls can be heard ahead, and the gorge holds some impressive falls and pools which are worth swimming. As the easy going valley path passes Rough Crag after about 3 kilometres of walking, it steepens, coming close to the gorge below, then levels out in the hanging valley above. Ahead can be seen the buttress of Great Lad Crag with the eroded fissures of Ladcrag Beck to its left.
**2.5 miles**

**2** At Ladcrag Beck the path veers roughly north, north-east and ascends through boulders and bracken to another hanging valley with yet more waterfalls and deep pools. After crossing Waver Beck, the ground becomes boggy but remains level and a prominent crag with a Y-shaped chimney can be seen on the spur to the north-east. Turn off the defined path leading steeply up to Little Lad Crag and cut under the crag with the Y-shaped chimney, and past the stone sheepfold.

The path here is very indistinct and difficult to follow but heads steadily north-east; navigate by the thin gill flowing down the broad shallow 'V' of the surrounding terrain, as it leads to the tarn above, passing on its way a very prominent, stunted pine tree. It is a relief after the hard hike up through the tussocky ground to crest the boggy boulder-strewn rim that contains Scoat Tarn. Scoat Tarn is an extremely rewarding place to swim after such a long walk in.
**1.2 miles**

**3** From the outflow of Scoat Tarn head due south for about 100 metres before bearing off to the east slightly heading towards the top of the lowest rocky mound ahead and the tiny pools of water there, which points out to the distant coast and the Ravenglass

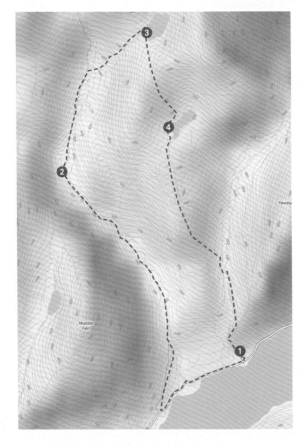

delta. The ground is rough and covered in beak sedge but is manageable and quite pleasant walking. Crest the broad spur emanating from Red Pike above, heading south, south-east descending down the side of the spur to Low Tarn and its attendant tarnlets. The view from the spur across the tarn is wonderful and takes in the broad expanse of Wast Water and its valley and even Burnmoor Tarn can be seen in splendid isolation on Eskdale Moor.

Not as dramatic at Scoat Tarn, Low Tarn is still a very worthy place for a swim, and after the effort of getting here it would be a shame to pass up such an opportunity.
**0.6 miles**

❹ At Low Tarn, walk around to the outflow, Brimfull Beck. There is a very indistinct trod which shadows the beck roughly south towards the prominent tor on the horizon. Stay on the broad high ground as the terrain descends to the south, south-east moving away from the beck and avoiding its re-entrant to the east. This route descends via the blunt feature of Knott Ends before cutting down south-east over steep, rough ground to reach the good valley path that follows Over Beck.

Once on the valley path, head down and over the two bridges over the beck, one new, one old. Carry on down the eastern side of the beck on the footpath which soon reaches the car park at Overbeck Bridge.
**1.9 miles**

Walk 23

# THE EMERALD POOL, SPRINKLING TARN AND STYHEAD TARN

Spouthead Gill is home to The Emerald Pool, a rare gem, together with Sprinkling and Styhead Tarn it provides a perfect day out for the mountain swimmer.

INFORMATION

DISTANCE: 7.1 miles
TIME: 6 hours
MAP: Harvey's British Mountain Map: Lake District, OS Explorer OL6 The English Lakes SW
START/END POINT: Wasdale Head Car Park (NY 186 084, CA20 1EX)
PUBLIC TRANSPORT: The nearest train station is Seascale, near Gosforth. Take a taxi from there. There are no buses to Wasdale Head.
SWIMMING: The Emerald Pool (NY 214 091), Sprinkling Tarn (NY 227 090), Styhead Tarn (NY 221 099)
PLACES OF INTEREST: St Olaf's Church, Eskdale Mill, Hardknott Castle Roman Fort, Ravenglass and Eskdale Railway
REFRESHMENTS: The Sawmill Cafe & Farm Shop, Nether Wasdale (019467 26716, CA20 1ET); Wasdale Head Inn, Wasdale Head (019467 26229, CA20 1EX).
EASIER ACCESS: Reasonable access on the north-western shore of Wast Water.
NEARBY SWIM SPOTS: Wast Water, Eskdale, Burnmoor Tarn, Blea Tarn at Beckfoot

Wasdale Head has provided the gateway to many a happy adventure for its visitors and no doubt a few fraught epics too. It is something of an adventure just to get there, particularly if you travel via the mountain passes of Wrynose and Hardknott. It is home to the highest mountain, the deepest lake, the smallest church and biggest liar in England; there is never a dull moment to be had there.

The highest mountain is easy to determine. At 978 metres, Scafell Pike along with the high peaks around it, dominate the skyline to the east of Wasdale Head and overshadow Wast Water below, our deepest lake at a cool 79 metres. The smallest church can be found at the beginning of this route and sure enough, St Olaf's Church is as small as it is ancient and is tucked away in its own yew-bordered grounds. The roof beams are thought to have come from Viking ships and the church has long been associated with British climbers, many of whom are buried in the churchyard after having met their fate in the surrounding mountains. The biggest liar is not so easy to work out and refers to the landlord of what was then the Wastwater Hotel in the 1800s and which is now the Wasdale Head Inn. Auld Will Ritson was what they called him and by all accounts he was an expert spinner of yarns and considered on his own insistence to be the biggest liar in England. Fascinating facts, but of course what we are really interested in is the swimming, and of that there is plenty.

Whichever route you take from Wasdale Head you will come upon some of the best mountaineering to be had in the land and some of the best water to boot. The lonesome Scoat Tarn and Low Tarn can be reached from Mosedale or just down the valley

via Nether Beck, and brooding Wast Water is close to hand, offering big lake swimming in a dramatic mountainous environment. This route however takes us straight to the head of the old mountain pass at Styhead and to the tarns there, via the road less-travelled. There is good reason for this, for nestled at the head of Lingmell Beck, where tributaries converge from Lingmell, Broad Grag and Great End, is the fabled Emerald Pool ❷.

A very good friend of mine alluded to the location of this pool many years ago, and I have been deeply grateful to him since. Swimming in the mountains is made special by the sheer variety and beauty of locations which change constantly with the seasons and the vagaries of the weather. Certain places can define a route and make it something unique and this is certainly the case with the Emerald Pool, lined as it is with boulders and pebbles of the green-blue volcanic rock so typical of this part of the Lakes.

This attractive coloured igneous rock was laid down during the Lower Palaeozoic period some 460 million years ago and is part of the Borrowdale Volcanic Group of greenstones, one of the three main belts of different rock types that are found in the Lake District. The minerals in these variegated forms of greenstone are what give the rock its colour. Interestingly, garnet-bearing rock is also to be found here. The immense heat and pressure of volcanic activity breaking the chemical bond in the rock caused its minerals to recrystallise, creating the semi-precious garnet stones. Another reason, if one was needed, to dive deep down into the cold clear waters of Lingmell Beck.

There are a series of pools and falls, each more attractive than the last, leading up and beyond the confluence of Spouthead and Piers Gills. Here the Emerald Pool lies with the falls gushing in from different angles at its head. Small, cold and beautiful, it sets a swimmer up for the day.

On leaving the beck and reaching the rim of Styhead Pass, one is firmly back on the path well-travelled. The brand new, shiny aluminium stretcher box at the head of the pass seems otherworldly in its rocky environment and holds something of a reassuring allure to passing hikers. Many of them sit around it for a break before heading off up to Great Gable or Scafell Pike. This is the latest instalment of a very fine history of mountain safety and rescue provision from times when there were no organised mountain rescue teams, and it was a case of climbers helping climbers if anyone got into trouble.

The plod up to Sprinkling Tarn ❸ is filled with anticipation as the path winds its way up one of the most impressive mountain ranges in England. The walk from the stretcher box to the tarn is about a kilometre and will take about half an hour for most walkers. Sprinkling Tarn is perfectly situated on the broad rocky saddle that emanates from Seathwaite Fell. The buttress of Great End, one of the five great summits of the Scafell range, soars above it to the south-west and there never was a more impressive place to take a swim. The tarn is roughly triangular in shape and bears a striking resemblance to a splashing fish when viewed on the map.

The domed rocky outcrops that surround the tarn show clear signs of ice scouring and there are some excellent examples of *roches moutonnée* to be found. Towards its northernmost tip, a promontory juts out across the tarn almost cutting across it completely, hiding from view the tiny island which lies next to the north-east shore. It is quite shallow a good way around the tarn with a sharp rocky bottom, the deepest part lies between the

south edge of the promontory and the centre of the main basin. In sunny weather it is a joy to take a swim before warming up and drying off on the rocks while watching the parade of hill walkers head off up The Band or passing on their way to Esk Hause.

*"It is not the pretty places – the flowery lanes of Grasmere, or Derwentwater's wooded bays - that keep him restless in his bed, it is the magnificent ones. Places like Great End…"* A Wainwright, *The Southern Fells.*

It is always a wrench to leave Sprinkling Tarn, captivating as it is, but Styhead Tarn ❹ is yet to be explored and the walk down to it is pleasant enough. The outflow from Sprinkling Tarn follows the path down before veering off to the north to join other little gills in flowing into the marshy delta at the head of Styhead Tarn. Like the previous tarn, Styhead is not a cirque tarn and has an open aspect with views of the vast fellscape which surrounds it. As a swimming spot it is not as endearing as some, but it is its location that makes it remarkable. The tarn is thought to be half the size that it once was due to the infilling effect of

deposits brought down from Sprinkling Tarn Beck and Aaron Slack, the effects of which can be seen during the walk down to the tarn.

The northern shore provides the best access to the water, where small, sharp, red rocks provide a less painful entry into the water between the larger rocks. In the shallower bays to the south of the tarn weeds and lilies perfuse the water pleasantly and the eyes are draw to the sunless cleft of Piers Gill to the south-west with the buttresses of the Scafell range towering overhead.

The walk back along Moses Trod follows the old dalesman route linking Seathwaite with Wasdale named after Moses Rigg, 18th-century slate man, illicit whisky distiller and plumbago smuggler (or is this just one of Auld Will Ritson's yarns?). This is the primary walking route for most folk entering the valley and although it can be busy, it is nice to have some company on the descent and the miles pass quickly in such rich surroundings. The warmth of the bar and a cool pint await at the Wasdale Head Inn ahead, where the joys of the day can be relived and plans for the next adventure discussed.

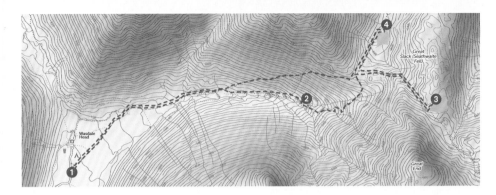

**1** From the car park at the rough track junction *before* the Wasdale Head Inn car park head up the track heading north-east, passing St Olaf's Church on the left. At Burnthwaite Farm, stay left at the barn and go through the gate following the track by the wall and continue through the gate then east along Moses Trod.

The path eventually leads over a narrow wooden bridge. Stay on the path heading east. 450 metres after the bridge the path forks. Take the gravel and grass path to the right which leads through the bracken and eventually the boggy ground by Lingmell Beck. Follow the path upstream for about 1 kilometre, passing through the gate in the wall as the path ascends towards the meeting of Spouthead and Peirs Gills. There is a small but prominent holly bush by the path, turn right towards the beck here to discover the pool.
**1.9 miles**

**2** From the pool, drop back downstream until the footpath that

runs down the obvious spur running down from Stand Crag can be reached by fording the stream. Follow this path as it steepens and zig-zags east, crossing the beck again as well as the upper reaches of Spounthead Gill further on, before the path heads to the north, north-west to join Styhead Pass at the stretcher box where good views towards Styhead Tarn can be enjoyed.

From the stretcher box take the gravel path heading east along the col and stay on this well-defined path as it gradually ascends. The path takes a turn to the south-east before levelling off as it reaches Sprinkling Tarn. There is good access all of the way around the tarn but the best basking rocks (should you be blessed with warm and sunny weather) lie above the north-west shoreline.
**1.2 miles**

**3** From Sprinkling Tarn retrace your steps back to the stretcher box at Styhead Pass then follow the main path north-east down to the tarn which lies very much in sight in

all but the thickest hill fog. The tarn is only 400 metres from the stretcher box and the descent is an easy one. The easiest entry is from the gravelly bay on the north shore.
**0.9 miles**

**4** From the tarn, retrace your steps back up to Styhead Pass and the stretcher box. Then take the Moses Trod path which drops down to the south-west before bearing off in a westerly direction under Great Gable, descending steeply all the way to the valley bottom.

The descent route is very easy to follow although it is steep, with the odd scramble to contend with along the way. As the path reaches more level ground there is some respite for the legs and the route rejoins our ascent route where the path nears Lingmell Beck. The same route is followed, through Burnthwaite Farm and back past St Olaf's Church to return to the car park. There is a shortcut footpath through to the pub at St Olaf's Church if you are in need of sustenance.
**2.5 miles**

# UPPER ESK AND SCAFELL PIKE

Two exceptional things in one walk: the upper Esk with its endless supply of perfect pools, and Scafell Pike, highest mountain in England, grim, steep and utterly irresistible.

## INFORMATION

DISTANCE: 10.5 miles
TIME: 9 hours
MAP: Harvey British Mountain Map: Lake District, OS Explorer OL6 The English Lakes SW
START/END POINT: Jubilee Bridge (NY 213 011)
PUBLIC TRANSPORT: Nearest train station is Seascale, near Gosforth, or Ravenglass. Narrow gauge train The La'al Ratty connects Ravenglass with Eskdale on the Ravenglass and Eskdale Railway. If travelling from Ambleside it is best to take a taxi. There are no bus services.
SWIMMING: The Esk Falls (NY 226 037), Tongue Pot (NY 226 035), Kail Pot (NY 217 023), Birk Dub (NY 215 021)
PLACES OF INTEREST: Wasdale Head, Hardknott Castle Roman Fort, Ravenglass and Eskdale Railway
REFRESHMENTS: The Boot Inn, Boot (019467 23711, CA19 1TG); Brook House Inn, Boot (019467 23288, CA19 1TG); Woolpack Inn – Hardknott Bar & café, Boot (019467 23230, CA19 1TH); Bower House Inn, Eskdale (019467 23244, CA19 1TD).
EASIER ACCESS: The swimming can be accessed easily by walking the route in reverse.
NEARBY SWIM SPOTS: Take advantage of the many swim opportunities along the upper River Esk, the Duddon Valley, Blea Tarn at Beckfoot, Stanley Force, Dalegarth Bridge.

irst a gentle warning: this is a walk for fit and experienced fell walkers, competent in navigation and at ease in the high mountain environment. Once past the more popular stretches of the River Esk, the route takes the path less-travelled and there will not be crowds of walkers to follow. The capable and adventurous swim-hiker will be rewarded with an unsurpassed mountain day, filled with memories of the most beautiful and dramatic places in England. All of the swimming can be accessed relatively easily, by beginning this route in reverse and just hiking along the river to the head of the valley (although the best fell walking is lacking), so no one need miss out on the swimming at least.

The first time I approached Scafell Pike ❹ via this route I experienced the ever present dilemma that lurks within the amphibian-human… stop and swim in the glistening pools or head to the soaring heights of the hills? By making an early start and taking the path to the west of the river via Damas Dubs, the decision is hopefully made easier by removing the temptation! This route aims to gain the great rocky summit of Scafell Pike first, before beginning the descent down the entire length of the upper River Esk. With this approach we can have our cake and eat it, using the return route as the ideal foil for a taxing hike and leaving time to do the pools and dubs of the Esk justice. This is not an experience to be rushed and there is a lot to be discovered.

The beginning of the walk quickly deviates away from the Esk to proceed along the edge of Damas Dubs. The Dubs are a boggy but atmospheric place and give tantalising glimpses of the mountains beyond Cam Spout Crag. Although wet underfoot and offering no swimming prospects, this route does offer peace and solitude away from the often busy route up to the more popular sections of the Esk and avoids the rather dangerous path that runs under Green Crag. It is highly probable that the next time fellow walkers are encountered will be on Scafell Pike summit.

Just before the ascent to Mickledore, Sampson's Stones come into view. These great boulders were plonked down here by receding glaciers and offer some of the best bouldering in the Lakes. They also offer a bit of interest and diversion prior to the steep climbing ahead and this is a good place to have a quick drink and adjust clothing accordingly, although as Wainwright notes, "there is no time for dawdling when bound for Scafell Pike".

The walk up past Cam Spout is best taken at a steady Himalayan plod, all the better to admire the impressive and constantly unfolding terrain. When compared to the falls of the River Esk, Cam Spout may not seem so impressive, but it is its location that lends it weight and whilst climbing the good path to its right, this can be appreciated to the full.

The walking above Cam Spout is heavy going and it is a relief to finally crest the col of Mickledore and to gaze down both sides of the saddle. Mickledore is an Old English expression for 'the great gap' and is a fine name for such a place. It links the two highest peaks in England, is home to a mountain rescue stretcher box and is an awe inspiring place to be. The walk to the rocky summit cone is fairly straight-forward from here in good weather, although in poor visibility a little bit of accurate navigation will be necessary. None of the paths leading to the summit can be said to be hard to follow in fair conditions, but in bad weather the terrain can be confusing, appearing as a jumble of rocks and cairns.

The summit of Scafell Pike is as it should be, a harsh place covered in rock, marked with a vast cairn, and almost always surrounded with proud and satisfied hikers, perhaps unaware that only half of the challenge is over. Once on a mist-wreathed autumn day early in the morning, I arrived at the summit which was already surrounded by a large group of Indian gentlemen. They insisted on brewing me up, from scratch, the best chai masala I have ever tasted. I couldn't thank them enough and I had a warm feeling in the pit of my stomach all the way back down to Wasdale.

One must always take care when leaving the summit to orient oneself so as to at least head off in the right direction. There is a lot of steep ground about and it pays to be on route. The path to the col leading to Broad Crag is straightforward if such precautions are taken and the steep descent down little Narrowcove beneath Pen and Dow Crag soon leads back to the headwaters of the Esk. The thought of some world-class dipping in crystal clear pools is enough to put a spring back in tired legs and it is a treat to have the company of the river again. Once over the bogs of Great Moss and past Scar Lathing the pools appear at the bases of the tumble of waterfalls cascading down the gorge by the path.

If you have never visited the upper Esk before you are in for a treat, concentrate your efforts on the Tongue Pot, Kail Pot and Birk Dub ❻. It is easy to become overwhelmed with choice as there are so many attractive places to dip and explore. To swim the bright pools, full of dappled little brown trout is the antithesis of the mountain experience with its brooding crags and mist-wreathed summits. The two complement each other well and if good time has been made during the day then a happy few hours can be spent in the water, with the knowledge that an easy walk along the valley bottom leads back home. Brew up if you have the means, and bask in the accomplishment of a grand day out, you have tasted the two extremes, and have come back smiling.

❶ From Jubilee Bridge, head west down the road to take the right turn north, along the track over Hardknott Gill heading towards the farm. Stay on the right of way that runs alongside the River Esk and turn left over the footbridge to arrive at Taw House. Take the right of way leading out of Taw House grounds heading to the north-east and follow this for a kilometre, over the fords by the small rills to Scale Bridge.

I mile

❷ Cross Scale Bridge and carry on the north-east path for 150 metres and take the path which cuts in steeply from the left heading west, north-west. This path zig-zags up the southern end of Brock Crag and leads onto the boggy plateau of Damas Dubs. Here the path follows an unnamed gill north-east for 300 metres before it turns to the north and begins to skirt the border of Damas Dubs proper. Stick to the path, it offers the best way ahead despite appearances.

As the path approaches the slopes of Rowantree Crags it takes an abrupt turn to the east before resuming a north, north-easterly track. Stay on this path for 2 kilometres as it passes beneath Silverybield Crag before heading north and joining the banks of the River Esk once more.

The path bears around to the north, north-west as it crosses a number of gills flowing from the fells to the left before reaching a sheepfold by the wall that comes straight down from Tom Fox's Crag above. Here the path takes a turn to the north-east and leads, in 200 metres, to Sampson's Stones, a collection of big boulders next to a little eyot in the river.

2.4 miles

❸ From the stones, follow the path north then slightly to the east as it passes under Cam Spout Crag, here the path forks. Take the north-west path heading steeply up the défilé to the north of the crag, past How Beck and Cam Spout itself. This 1.5 kilometre climb leads up to the col of Mickledore which links Sca Fell with Scafell Pike and follows the line of least resistance along the series of re-entrants leading to the col. The path runs in a north-westerly direction, backing around to the north, north-west as it steepens to Mickledore.

Ascend the Mickledore ridge to the east, north-east and navigate carefully. The rocky path (well-furnished with cairns) leads up the rocky slopes leading to the vast summit cairn and trig point.

1.7 miles

❹ From Scafell Pike summit, again, carefully navigate off the summit dome in a north-easterly direction, down the rocky slabs towards Broad Crag. Stop at the col before ascending to Broad Crag and head right, steeply down the scree and into the broad gulley that holds Little Narrowcove Beck.

The path levels out slightly before descending steeply to the Bield at the confluence of Little Narrowcove and the young River Esk.

I mile

❺ From the confluence the path follows a relatively straight contour heading south-west, mirroring the route of the Esk below it. I kilometre on from the confluence the path meets How

Beck, a tributary of the Esk flowing down from the ascent route up to Mickledore. Don't cross the beck but take the path to the left which heads south-east to cross the Esk to carry on roughly south over the flat and boggy expanse of Great Moss, curving in slightly to follow the course of the river.

The path continues to follow the course of the river around to the east as it leads beneath Scar Lathing before taking an abrupt turn to the right to head south, south-west following the wide gorge containing the upper Esk Waterfalls. From the sharp turn stay on the boggy path for a kilometre all the way past Throstlehow Crag and down to the picturesque Lingcove Bridge. **2.5 miles**

**6** From Lingcove Bridge follow the easy-to-follow path next to the River Esk along its entirety, back to Brotherilkeld and Jubilee Bridge. There is a high path and a low path. To take in all of the delights of the Esk, remain on the low river path which takes in Kail Pot and Birk Dub as detailed in this route

If you want to get back as soon as you can after exploring the pools of the upper Esk and Tongue Pot then take the detour onto the high path which leaves the river path route to gain higher ground about one kilometre south, south-west from Tongue Pot. **1.9 miles**

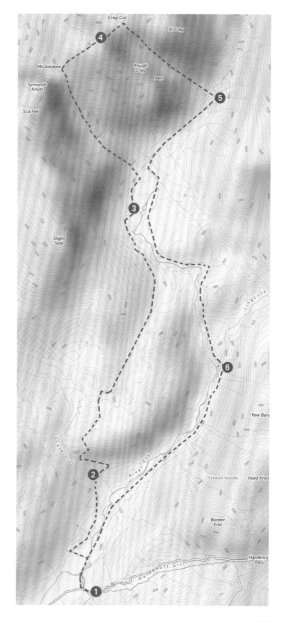

177

# Walk 25

# BLEA TARN AT BECKFOOT

A lovely walk from Dalegarth Station with good swimming at the tarn, and more waterfall pools than you can shake a stick at!

## INFORMATION

**DISTANCE:** 6.5 miles
**TIME:** 7 hours
**MAP:** Harvey's British Mountain Map: Lake District, OS Explorer OL6 The English Lakes SW
**START/END POINT:** Dalegarth Station (NY 173 007, CA19 1TG)
**PUBLIC TRANSPORT:** There are no buses to Eskdale. 'La'al Ratty', the Ravenglass and Eskdale Railway, runs between the two stations. Nearest mainline station is Ravenglass.
**SWIMMING:** Blea Tarn (NY 165 009), Whillan Beck Force (NY 181 020), Gill Force (NY 178 001), Stanley Force (NY 174 994), Dalegarth Bridge (NY 171 003)
**PLACES OF INTEREST:** Ravenglass and Eskdale Railway, Hardknott Castle Roman Fort, Eskdale Mill, Muncaster Castle, Eskdale Golf Course
**REFRESHMENTS:** The Boot Inn, Eskdale (019467 23711, CA19 1TG); Brook House Inn, Boot (019467 23288, CA19 1TG); Woolpack Inn - Hardknott Bar & café, Boot (019467 23230, CA19 1TH); Bower House Inn, Eskdale (019467 23244, CA19 1TD)
**NEARBY SWIM SPOTS:** Wast Water, Upper Esk Valley, Eel Tarn and Stony Tarn, Burnmoor Tarn, Devoke Water

This walk weaves in and around one of the best locations for wild swimming in the Lake District and includes tarn swimming, multiple waterfall pools and some lovely deep river glides. There is so much to fit in that it may be sensible for some swim hikers to break the route up into two parts as suggested in the directions. Aside from the exceptional swimming and dipping opportunities there are the La'al Ratty steam trains running along the Ravenglass and Eskdale Railway to explore, as well as Eskdale Mill and some very fine pubs. All of which are very distracting from the task in hand, but my advice would be to make the most of any good weather that comes your way and never waste an opportunity to swim and explore.

The first of our swims lies just up on the fell above the station, and although the going is steep, it doesn't take too much effort to get to. Blea Tarn ❷ was formed by glacial moraine from Scafell which was deposited around the rough granite outcrops that surround it. The tarn is enclosed on three sides by small heather-covered outcrops and is open to the south-west with excellent views over Muncaster Fell and on towards the estuary at Ravenglass. It holds clear, sweet water and has pleasant grassy banks on its open side and is the perfect place for a swim after the efforts of scaling the steep Hollinghead Bank. Nearby and to the west are Siney Tarn and Blind Tarn which are handsome tarns in their own right but are unfortunately a little shallow for swimming.

Walking away from the tarn and up Bleatarn Hill the views become even more expansive. Scafell and Great Gable can be seen to the north-east, looking unfamiliar from this direction, and Eel Tarn and the prominent Harter Fell can be seen towards the east. On a clear day, the Isle of Man is clearly visible over

the sea to the west. The boggy path that leads off the fell, past the old mine shafts and buildings, is thoughtfully cairned, although it would only be necessary to use them in very poor visibility. Once back down in the valley bottom, one may question the purpose of heading off up Whillan Beck after such a perfect little walk, but it is worth bearing the extra miles if you have a love of waterfall pools.

The beck at the old mill at Gill Bank ❸ glides and bubbles into colourful shallow pools and belies what is to be found just 200 metres upstream. Here the full power of the stream is unleashed at Whillan Beck Force, which creates its own downdraft in the dark deep pool below. It is a place to take the breath away in every sense of the word and elicits the same response in every swimmer I have taken there: wide eyes and a broad grin.

The building at Gill Bank was a carding mill and still has its old wheel and well-constructed leat leading from the beck. Carding mills prepared wool by brushing them into rolls for spinning or batting for quilts and this one was perfectly situated for both power and wool from the nearby farms. The path from the farm at Gill Bank leads to another, still working mill at the bottom of the bank. Eskdale Mill is an old corn mill with a fully-functioning wheel and mill and has a delightful rocky mill pool downstream from the wheel. If there is time it is certainly worth a visit, bearing in mind that there is still a lot of swimming to be done!

The final looping tour of the valley takes in Gill Force ❺, the 60-foot ribbon-like falls of Stanley Force and the pools under the Dalegarth Bridge. This provides a veritable glut of perfect waterfall pools and pebbled glides for the swimmer, so much so that it is inconceivable that anyone would want to miss out on swimming them. Full marks to anyone swimming every spot on this route however, it is a big day out if all of the swimming locations are to be fully appreciated and may add to the suggested time taken for the route. Pack light and leave early to get the most from it.

❶ From the station car park, head out onto the road and turn right heading west, south-west towards Beckfoot. At Beckfoot Bridge Station, cross the narrow gauge tracks and go through the unsigned gate and follow the grassy path that heads up the fell past the little copse on the right.

Continue up the steep zig-zagging grassy path through the bracken, which trends on a north-westerly direction for about a kilometre. Don't be tempted to follow one of the offshoot paths which head directly west. As the path levels out somewhat, the lumpy contours at the head of Hollinghead Bank come into view. Blea Tarn is just around the corner to the north-west of the hillocks. The southern shoreline has a couple of nice grassy edges with just enough shingle between the sharp rocks to spare bare feet.
**0.9 miles**

❷ From the south shore of the tarn, follow the path that runs alongside the eastern shore beneath the hillocks. Stay on this sinuous, boggy path heading north-east and up onto the eastern flank of Bleatarn Hill. From Bleatarn Hill the cairned path descends in a north-easterly direction through boggy ground, passing the old iron mine shafts along the way.

About a kilometre from Bleatarn Hill, the path turns to the east and passes some well-made stone mine buildings, before curving around to the south as it cuts

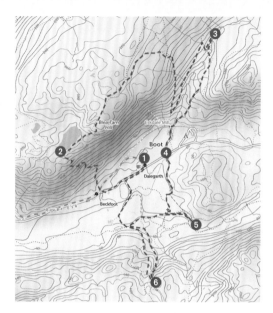

down and across Boot Bank, past a network of wall and sheep folds. Just before the bridge that leads to Boot village, take the path through the gate on the left and follow the wall north-east alongside Whillan Beck.

The path gently ascends through three gates as the terrain levels out and becomes more open, with juniper and larch dotted about. After the third gate, follow the path to the right which zig-zags down to the old mill by the bridge at Gill Bank Farm. To get to the waterfall, pass through the kissing gate and follow the trod through the mill grounds, heading upstream in the direction of the mill leat, over the stile and the awkward ground ahead for

about 200 metres. Here you will be rewarded with the sight of Whillan Beck Force and its deep pool. Take care on the steep ground and heed the 'Danger, No Diving' sign.
**2.1 miles**

❸ From the falls head back to the bridge at the mill and cross it to pass through the gates at Gill Bank Farm. Stay on the farm track that leads all the way down to Bridge End Farm and Eskdale Mill at Boot with its lovely mill pool and working wheel. Carry on through the village to the main road at the Brook House Inn.
**0.9 miles**

❹ At Brook House Inn you can either turn right and head back to

Dalegarth, which is only 200 metres down the road, and finish early, or carry on directly across the road following the right of way to Esk View Farm. Just past the farm buildings the track hooks to the right and immediately crosses a T-junction of walled tracks. Carry on over the junction and take the next bridleway on the left heading south. Keep on going as the path meets another from the right, until you reach the river. Cross the river by the stepping stones and turn left to follow the river bank east. After 200 metres the river bends then another 200 metres will lead you to Gill Force.
**0.6 miles**

**5** From Gill Force, go back the way you came to the stepping stones. Keep on straight ahead, following the river west. Cross Stanley Gill at the ford and take the track to the small tarn in the woods. Take the first path on the left which zigs back at a sharp angle towards the gill. Follow this path uphill for about 600 metres as it winds its way alongside and over the gill, all the way up to the spectacular Stanley Force.
**1 mile**

**6** From Stanley Force either retrace your steps to the small tarn in the woods or take the alternative footpath down through the woods to return to the same place. All of the northward paths from the waterfall end up by the track next to the small tarn so don't worry too much if you feel you have gone off route.

From the track by the tarn, head north-west around the outskirts of the wood to get to the car park. Keep going the short distance to Dalegarth Bridge to enjoy the last swim of the day at the lovely pool there.
**0.6 miles**

**7** From the bridge, follow the road north to meet the main road again, then turn right and return to the car park at Dalegarth Station.
**0.4 miles**

# THE DUDDON VALLEY AND SEATHWAITE TARN

This is a wonderful walk up to the seldom-visited Seathwaite Tarn with a return via the enchanting River Duddon and its wooded pools.

## INFORMATION

DISTANCE: 7.7 miles
TIME: 6 hours
MAP: Harvey British Mountain Map: Lake District, OS Explorer OL6 The English Lakes SW
START/END POINT: Froth Pot Bridge Car Park (SD 235 995)
PUBLIC TRANSPORT: Nearest train station is Seascale, near Gosforth, or Ravenglass. From here or if travelling from Ambleside it is best to take a taxi. There are no bus services.
SWIMMING: Seathwaite Tarn (SD 253 989), River Duddon at Birks Bridge (SD 234 993), Froth Pot (SD 234 995)
PLACES OF INTEREST: Wasdale Head, Hardknott Castle Roman Fort, Ravenglass and Eskdale Railway
REFRESHMENTS: Newfield Inn in Seathwaite is a very good traditional pub (01229 716208, LA20 6ED). The Broughton-in-Furness Village Bakery (01229 716284, LA20 6HQ) is excellent and there are good cafes and pubs there too.
NEARBY SWIM SPOTS: River Esk, Coniston Water, Devoke Water

To enter the Duddon Valley during the quiet times of the year is to step back in time to a gentler pace of life. It is easy to imagine Wordsworth by the stepping stones, musing on the virtues of the river which he knew and loved well from his childhood. He wrote extensively about the Duddon and in 1820 published *The River Duddon: A Series of Sonnets*. He certainly did the Duddon proud, although his reviewers were perplexed as to why he should write about such an insignificant river with an ugly name. One can imagine a wry smile spreading across William's face as he read his reviews – the Duddon is one of the finest rivers in England!

*And thou, blue streamlet, murmuring yield'st no more*
*Than a soft record that whatever fruit*
*Of ignorance thou mightst witness heretofore,*
*Thy function was to heal and to restore,*
*To soothe and cleanse, not madden and pollute!*

From *The River Duddon: A Series of Sonnets* – William Wordsworth

The River Duddon rises 1,289 feet above sea level by the Three Shire Stone at the head of the Wrynose Pass. Here the old counties of Cumberland, Lancashire, and Westmorland meet. The Duddon marks the boundary between Cumberland and Lancashire as it tumbles and meanders (as all rivers should) through the Duddon Valley before entering the Irish Sea at Duddon Sands. A renowned trout and salmon river, it is also host to many other beloved species including the kingfisher, the otter and at Duddon Sands, the rare natterjack toad.

Aside from its wonderful river the Duddon Valley, also known as Dunnerdale, allows good access to the more secluded walking in the less visited areas of the Cumberland fells to the west and the Furness Fells of Lancashire to the east: the Ulpha and Dunnerdale Fells, Harter Fell and Grey Friar all offer solitude in magnificent settings. It also is home to the extensive Dunnerdale Forest, and attractive mixed woodland lines the river banks, at least below Cockley Beck. Dunnerdale is a haven for wildlife; buzzards and peregrine falcons fly overhead and red squirrels can be found in the woods. Ulpha (whose name derives from an early word for wolf), used to be home to an extensive deer park and the deer still roam the forests and fells. In the spring and summer months the fields and hedgerows are decorated with bluebells, violets, primroses and wood anemones.

Outdoor swimmers, if perusing a map of the area (an obsession of the author), will be drawn to the expanse of blue nestled up in the Seathwaite Fells. Seathwaite Tarn ❷ lies in a glorious setting sandwiched between the steeps of Dow Crag and Shudderstone How to the south and Grey Friar and Goat Crag to the north. The tarn lies in a glacial trough at the gateway to a double headed valley. Raven Nest How stands guard at the entrance to the remote upper valleys, which are open and inviting by comparison and hide the paths that descend from Levers and Goat's Hawse, the two most significant cols emanating from the Old Man of Coniston to the east.

The tarn is 1,200 metres long and 300 metres wide, and its maximum depth was measured by the Brathay Exploration Group at just over 29 metres. The tarn gets shallower towards its extreme ends, and it has one tiny island on the north-west shore, where cormorants, black headed gulls and Canada geese can sometimes be found loitering, depending on the time of year.

The old levels of Seathwaite Copper Mine, which was active up until the mid-19th century, lie above the head of the tarn. The mine appears as a location in the novel *The Plague Dogs* by Richard Adams, where the two canine heroes Rowf and Snitter shelter and form an alliance with a wily fox, or the Tod (as Adams calls him), before continuing their escape.

In 1907 the Barrow Corporation enlarged the tarn with a dam to create a reservoir for the town's water supply, supplementing the water it takes from the River Duddon. This raised the level of the original tarn by 6 metres (and what a special place that must have been before the dam). The water is abstracted from the off-take weir at the south-west shore, while the outflow of the enchanting Tarn Beck flows on beneath. There are some deep pools below Black Allens, the hillock beneath the dam, and some nice cascades further on, and this this route attempts to follow the course of Tarn Beck as closely as possible, in order to fully appreciate it.

Our descent along the course of the beck travels through some lovely country including Turner Hall Farm and its welcoming campsite near the base of the Walna Scar Road. The campsite here is how all campsites used to be, just a field set in beautiful surroundings, with basic but very well maintained facilities and comes highly-recommended.

Just along from Turner Hall Farm is the village of Seathwaite and the famous Newfield Inn ❹. Famous for its association with William and Dorothy Wordsworth, who arrived to stay at the inn after hiking over the Walna Scar Road from Coniston in 1804. Also, exactly a century later in

1904, it was the scene of a riot caused by 50 Irish navvies who were working on the Seathwaite Tarn dam. The drinking began at 10am and things had got out of hand by the evening. They began to smash the bar up after being asked to leave and the landlord and his men had to resort to firearms to protect their lives and property; one person was killed, and another lost his leg. Not the average night out at the Newfield.

The Newfield Inn is a genuine countryman's pub. Dogs and boots are welcome, the ale is good, as is the food and the extraordinary floor features Walna Scar's finest slate. There is a spacious beer garden for warm days and there are regular folk music evenings. Combine this with a stay at the campsite and you have the makings of a perfect expedition.

From Seathwaite the return journey follows the course of the River Duddon and skirts the edge of Dunnerdale Forest. The river holds many pools as well as picturesque stepping stones and footbridges, none can compare with Birks Bridge and the pool beneath, near the end of this walk. The name of the bridge is a corruption of 'birch', there being a good population of birch trees in the area and the bridge is thought to date from the 18th century. It is a Grade II listed building and is exceptional in that, although man-made, it blends seamlessly with its environment. The series of drain holes set in its parapets also sets it apart, as do the quality of the voussoirs (the tapered stones used to construct an arch). Perhaps of more interest to the swimmer however, is the perfect pool which fills the small gorge underneath the bridge. Although shaded by trees, as a setting for a swim, it is hard to beat and makes a perfect finale to a day of swim-hiking, knowing that the car is parked just round the corner.

**1** From the car park near the modern bridge at Froth Pot (often called Birks Bridge Car Park, Birks Bridge is the stone packhorse bridge further downstream), head out onto the road, turning left to head north-east. 250 metres up the road a forestry track cuts up through the woods at the same angle as the road, follow this track for 150 metres and take the footpath on the right which heads off in a south-westerly direction.

The path soon bears around to the south and reaches a wall, follow the path alongside the wall until it reaches a gate as the path exits the wood. Cut south-east across the meadow to the wall and follow the path, through the gate in the wall and into the next meadow heading south. As the wall begins to bear downhill the path cuts through the wall and heads up the fell to the east following the course of Tarn Beck, the outflow of Seathwaite Tarn. Stay to the north of the beck on the path as it gradually ascends to the shore of Seathwaite Tarn. Anywhere along the shoreline is good to swim.
**1.8 miles**

**2** From the tarn shore head south-west back along the shoreline to the gantry style footbridge. In order to fully explore the falls of the Tarn Beck, break away from the track leading on from the footbridge and head across the fell to the west, following the direction of the beck as it meanders over fairly level ground until it reaches Foss How, negotiate the wall here

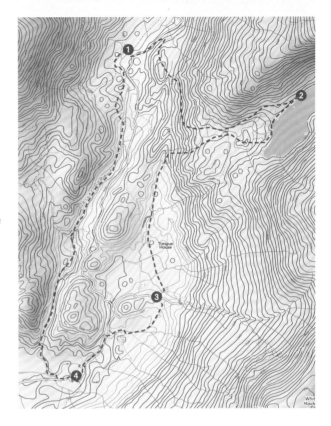

and carry on. At Foss How the beck cascades down the hill before taking an abrupt turn to the south, south-west just before this change of direction a path crosses the beck, following the retaining wall and the course of the water. Stay on this path for a kilometre as it crosses a series of meadows and walls, always following the course of Tarn Beck.

As the path approaches the Togue House buildings it is channelled

into the yard and becomes a track. Carry on through the yard between the buildings, ignoring the path off to the right that heads over the footbridge. Stay on the path that cuts across the meadows and Sunny Pike Gill heading south, south-east.

From Tongue House to the next set of buildings at Long House is just over 500 metres, carry on across the meadows and through the gates to Long House. Just

before the yard at Long House a track heads off to the south-west over Long House Gill, follow this to its junction with the road.
**2.2 miles**

❸ From the Long House road junction cut straight across the road to follow the footpath opposite. Follow this path through a series of meadows and walls as it gradually bears around to the west and arrives at Turner Hall Farm and its lovely campsite. Stay on the track as it passes the farm to arrive at the road.

At the road turn left, heading south, south-west along the winding road to the sharp turn to the right which brings you to the village of Seathwaite and, just down the road the wonderful Newfield Inn.
**1 mile**

❹ Tear yourself away from the Newfield Inn and carry on down the road to the west for just over 100 metres. Follow the footpath over the bridge to cross the Tarn Beck for the last time. Follow the wooded path west along the bank of the beck until in reaches the River Duddon and carry on to the foot bridge. Cross the bridge to the west bank path which heads out of the woods and follows the Duddon heading north, north-east beneath Wallowbarrow Crag. The path passes through attractive mixed woodland as it begins to gently climb away from the river. Just over a kilometre from the footbridge the path crosses Grassguards Gill.

Stay on the footpath heading north, north-east as the path re-joins the steep banks of the river. Stay on this path for another 1.5 kilometres, keeping right at the fork, until it finally emerges from the great Dunnerdale Forest. Follow the permissive path north as it picks up

and runs alongside a forest track at Great Wood which emerges at the delightful Birk's Bridge and its pool.

Follow the path upstream as it bends around to Froth Pot and cross the modern bridge to the car park.
**2.7 miles**

*Walk 27*

# CONISTON LAUNCH ADVENTURE

Boats, walking and swimming go so well together!
The Coniston Launch broadens the swimming
possibilities on Coniston Water, offering a perfect
day out for the adventurous swimmer.

oniston Water is a fascinating lake and not just because
of its wonderful setting. It has so many literary, artistic
and adventurous associations that there is something
here for everyone. Poets and artists will be drawn to
Brantwood, home of art critic and political philosopher John
Ruskin, and the Ruskin Museum. Parents and children alike will
be thrilled by the prospect of visiting Wild Cat Island and the
Octopus Lagoon of *Swallows and Amazons* fame. Motorsports
enthusiasts will be enthralled by the tales of Donald Campbell's
exploits in *Bluebird* and his ill-fated water speed record attempt.
For historians, fossil and mineral hunters, the fells surrounding
the lake still bear the age-softened scars of centuries of mining
and mineral extraction and are open and accessible for exploration. Fell walkers will head to these same fells that were also
home to Harry Griffin's Coniston Tigers, who trailblazed the
British mountaineering scene in the depressed 1930s. Surely this
is a list of attributes to excite even the most world-weary Lake
District tourist?

Let us lay aside Coniston's high profile historical associations for one moment. As a large body of water, it is eminently
attractive to the swimmer. Although justifiably popular, it is a
relatively safe place to swim. The 10mph speed limit and limited
access to power boats significantly reduces the danger posed
to the swimmer and it lacks the careless gin palace pilots often
encountered on Windermere. When on the water one only needs
to maintain a watchful eye on the Coniston Launch route and
the timetable of the wonderful Steam Yacht Gondola (the most
elegant way to get run over if ever there was one) in order to

## INFORMATION

**DISTANCE:** 5 miles
**TIME:** 5 hours
**MAP:** Harvey's British Mountain
Map: Lake District, OS Explorer OL6
The English Lakes SW. The Lake
District National Park's 'Map and
Guide to Coniston Water' is available
on their website.
**START/END POINT:** Coniston Launch
Jetty, Lake Road, Coniston (SD 307
970, LA21 8AN).
**PUBLIC TRANSPORT:** Nearest train
station in Windermere. The 505 bus
links Coniston to Ambleside and
Windermere. The X12 bus links
Coniston with Ulverston on the
Cumbrian coast rail line.
**SWIMMING:** Along the north-west
shore of Coniston Water (SD 298
939) and over to Peel Island from
Oxen House Bay (SD 291 919).
**PLACES OF INTEREST:** Brantwood
House, Ruskin Museum, The Coniston
Copper Mines, The Steam Yacht
Gondola, Coniston Boating Centre
(boat hire), Grizedale Forest (mountain
bike trails and Go Ape)
**REFRESHMENTS:** The Bluebird Café
(015394 41649, LA21 8AN); Swallows
and Amazons Tearoom at Bank
Ground Farm (01539441264, LA21
8AA); The Black Bull (015394 41335,
LA21 8DU); The Wilson's Arms,
Torver, good pub and deli (015394
41237, LA21 8BB)
**EASIER ACCESS:** Good access to the
lakeshore from The Bluebird Café.
**NEARBY SWIM SPOTS:** Goats
Water, Levers Water and Low Water,
Tarn Hows, Torver Common Tarn

ensure relative safety. The lake attracts mainly family paddlers (on SUPs, kayaks and canoes), sailors and swimmers.

For this route we rely heavily on the Coniston Launch Company. Their excellent service runs throughout the year, and they have heated cabins in the winter months (good for spring and autumn season diehards). The Coniston Launch operates various tours and routes on the lake along with very flexible tickets, allowing passengers to hop on and off at various locations around the lake. At the time of writing the Yellow Route Ticket will take you from their pier at Coniston to Sunny Bank via Torver. Sunny Bank is ideally situated to begin a walk to the lakeshore where our first swim is located. Following a little swimming adventure over to the island, this leaves the option to either take our proposed return walk along the Coniston Water shoreline, or to jump back on the next launch and return via Brantwood to Coniston.

The short walk across Torver Back Common leads to the rocky shoreline opposite Peel Island ❸, the only significant island on the lake worth a visit and a perfect one at that. Peel Island may have provided the inspiration for Authur Ransome's Wildcat Island (along with Blake Holme on Windermere) in his book, *Swallows and Amazons*. Ransome based the book loosely around his relationship with the Altounyan family and their children and the adventures they enjoyed together while sailing in their dinghies 'Swallow' and 'Mavis'. Bank Ground Farm, where the Altounyan family stayed the summer before *Swallows and Amazons* was written, is generally accepted to be the original Holly Howe. Here the fictional Walker family stayed on holiday as guests of the Jacksons. Peel Island, as well as Bank Ground Farm, were used as locations in the 1974

film adaptation (Peel Island also made an appearance in the 2016 remake of the film).

I had the pleasure of making the acquaintance of, and swimming with, Mr Martin Altounyan not so long ago. It was a pleasure to spend time with him in the water and he was very patient with my many questions regarding his family history. Ransome based his character of Roger on Martin's father, and his grandfather Ernest was Ransome's good friend, providing the connection between him and the family.

The draw Peel Island exerts on middle-aged parents is astonishing. Every summer wide-eyed adults can be found frantically exploring the island accompanied by bewildered children of varying ages who have had Ransome's story thrust upon them. All having a thoroughly good time of course, which is the whole point and lovely to witness. Although an extensive knowledge of Swallows and Amazons lore is not essential prior to this swim, it certainly adds to the excitement.

The swim out to the island is just under 400 metres and one must run the gauntlet of the launches on the lake during the crossing, but it is a very rewarding swim. Along with the anticipation of arriving on the island, the views towards The Old Man of Coniston and Dow Crag make this a unique adventure. On the way across, it is also interesting to point out that you will be swimming over the place where Donald Campbell crashed and died whilst travelling at 328mph in *Bluebird* in his attempt to beat the water speed record in 1967!

*Swallows* fan or not, the swim across the ribbon lake of Coniston and into the Secret Harbour of Wildcat Island is always a thrill. The dead holly leaves on the island can play havoc with bare feet, so take a pair of shoes over with you in your tow

float and perhaps a bottle of grog, so that you may explore the island when you arrive – it really is worth an explore. In Ransome's day there was still evidence of the ancient copper smelting works that were located here. Alas, they exist no more, but are well-documented in the Ruskin Museum. There is a good jump off the tallest of the rocks at the southernmost tip of the island and a circumnavigating swim around the island reveals the elephantine rocks surrounding it that are barely submerged. A swim towards the eastern shore of Coniston leads to High Peel Near, Low Peel Near and the pretty bay in-between them. This adds a bit of mileage to the swim but is worth the extra effort if you have it in you, and there are plenty of places to stop and admire the view along the way

The walk back to Coniston follows the Cumbria Way and offers a chance to see the water from a different perspective and to stop and swim at will. As is the case on most Cumbrian lakes, almost anywhere along the shoreline makes for good swimming, but Torver Common Wood provides a good backdrop to a swim as well as providing good picnicking ground.

Once back at Coniston, there is ample opportunity to recover from the adventure in one of the many good cafés and pubs. Ransome fans will of course be drawn to the other side of the lake to visit the Swallows and Amazons Tearooms at Bank Ground Farm, which is a very fitting way to finish the day, and which incidentally also has direct access to the lake – time for one more swim perhaps?

**1** Take the Coniston Launch from the pier (departure times begin at 10:00 and run every 90 minutes or so until 15:20). The trip to Sunny Bank takes 25 minutes and is a relaxing trip that allows an advanced recce of potential swimming spots along the way.
**0.9 miles**

**2** From the landing stage head south-west along the Cumbria Way across Torver Back Common. Turn left where the path meets the road and continue with care down the road, past Sunny Bank Mill, to the lake. Carry on along the road to the long lay-by where it is possible to scramble down to the edge of the lake exactly opposite Peel Island.

The getting in along the shore here is hard on the feet because of the rocks, but the water gets deep fairly quickly. Head for the middle of the island and use a tow float for the crossing, looking out for boats all the way. The 'Secret Harbour' is about two-thirds of the way along the island from the left, or northern end, and it gives the best access to the island's steep shore. Once on the island, head up and over the small ridge to explore the central clearing and rocky outcrops.

Continue the swim around the island and on to the east shore of the lake and continue on to the handsome bay between High and Low Peel Near. Return to Oxen House Bay the same way, exercising the same precautions.
**0.9 miles**

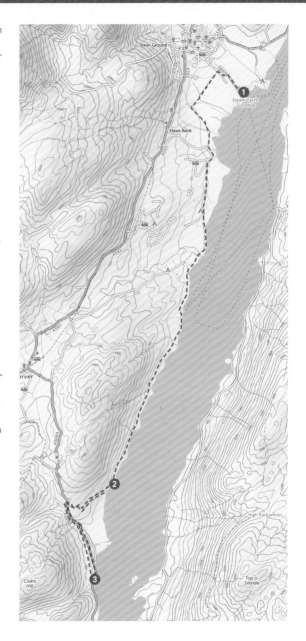

**3** From the bay, return to Sunny Bank landing stage by the same route. Carry on along the Cumbria Way, which hugs the shoreline heading north, north-east all the way back to Coniston. About 1.5 kilometres along from Sunny Bank the path reaches Moor Gill Foot. Anywhere between here and the Torver Coniston Launch lading

stage is a good place for more swimming in the shadow of Torver Common Wood.

The path continues on past the Torver landing and the jetty at Hoathwaite all the way to Water Park. Here the path leaves the shore as it passes through the campsite at Coniston Hall. Stay on

the Cumbria Way path all the way, ignoring the footpaths on the left just past Coniston Hall.

At Bowmanstead the Cumbria Way path takes a distinct right angle turn to the north-east. Follow this to Lake Road and return to Coniston Pier.
**4.1 miles**

# BLIND TARN, GOAT'S WATER AND TRANEARTH POOL

This adventure visits the best swimming spots in Coniston, the water is always baltic, but is a clear, slate blue colour and mesmerising to swim in.

T he fells that lie about The Old Man of Coniston are old and rounded; the soft outline of the land contrasting with the man-made intrusions into the rock and earth. In places the slate spoil heaps look as sharp and as fresh as the day they were split from the face of the rock, in other places they appear as ancient, warped, moss-covered shapes. Dow Crag alone stands out on the skyline above, looking like a crenellated fortress standing guard over Goat's Water. This walk avoids the often crowded routes that emanate from the beginning of the Walna Scar Road, at least until meeting it for a short while on the ascent to Blind Tarn, and for most of the way takes the path less-travelled.

The prized slate found here was formed during the Lower Palaeozoic era, just shy of 500 million years ago. Ordovician slate is silver-grey in colour which lightens the scenery and brightens the tarns and river pools that form and flow here. Ash Gill gives its name to this type of stratified rock, which is known as Ashgillian Shale. And if it is water you want, then this is the right place to be; even after prolonged dry spells it seems that water continues to permeate: cascading, dripping and seeping everywhere. A friendly warning – it is a real challenge to keep your feet dry on this route. The indistinct, boggy paths of Torver High Common laugh in the face of hiking boots but they will lead you beside tumbling becks lined with rowan, twisted ash, juniper and birch, past heather and holly and seemingly endless plains of rush and sphagnum. It is like walking through the fairy glen, or a set from *A Midsummer Night's Dream*.

Ancient quarry workings lie everywhere, testament to the rich copper seams formed between a land forged by supervolcanoes millions of years ago. Stone circles and ancient dwellings

## INFORMATION

DISTANCE: 7.7 miles
TIME: 6 hours
MAP: Harvey British Mountain Map: Lake District, OS Explorer OL6 The English Lakes SW
START/END POINT: Torver Village Hall Car Park (SD 284 942, LA21 8AZ)
PUBLIC TRANSPORT: Train station at Windermere, then 505 bus via Ambleside to Torver. The Blueworks X12 bus links Torver with Ulverston on the Cumbrian Coast rail line.
SWIMMING: Blind Tarn (SD 262 967), Goat's Water (SD 266 975), Tranearth Pool (SD 277 959), please note warnings below.
PLACES OF INTEREST: Coniston Copper Mines, The Ruskin Museum, Brantwood House, The Steam Yacht Gondola, Coniston Boating Centre
REFRESHMENTS: The Wilsons Arms in Torver is a good pub with an excellent deli attached (015394 41237, LA21 8BB). Swallows and Amazons Tearoom at Bank Ground Farm has something for everyone and great food on the east side of the lake (015394 41264, LA21 8AA). The Bluebird Café (015394 41649, LA21 8AN); The Black Bull (LA21 8DU, 015394 41335) and many more cafés, restaurants and pubs in Coniston.
EASIER ACCESS: Good access to the lakeshore from The Bluebird Café at the end of Lake Road.
NEARBY SWIM SPOTS: Coniston Water, Levers Water and Low Water, Tarn Hows

have been found all around this area, including ancient human remains and medieval bloomeries where iron and other ores were smelted in basic charcoal furnaces. Copper mining began in earnest here during the 16th century when Elizabeth I exploited the riches to be found in the local deposits, employing experts from the Tyrol and Bavaria. Copper mining continued to shape the local fells for centuries and ended in 1914, leaving the captivating landscape we see today, albeit softened with a cloak of moss and turf. There is an otherworldly atmosphere here of a once busy place, now empty, yet crowded with the ghosts of millennia.

The boggy crossing of Torver High Common leads eventually to the Walna Scar Road ❷, a much less squelchy prospect and a good navigational handrail in poor visibility. The Walna Scar Road follows the route of least resistance between Coniston and the Duddon Valley. It is one of the very old mountain passes in Cumbria that has remained in almost continuous use since our early history. Although it is a rough track, it was used by the carts of miners and quarrymen well into the 20th century and more recently I have seen it used to good effect by the mountain rescue team Land Rovers too. Now of course it is mainly used for recreational hiking and provides the best means of traversing the Coniston Fells to get to the many walking, climbing and swimming routes in the area.

Just off the Walna Scar Road lies the seldom visited Blind Tarn ❸. This is a real gem of a cirque tarn with very pleasing circular shape and is held in place by a thin moraine on its east side, with the vaulted heights of Brown Pike forming its back wall to the west. The basin of the tarn is very uniform in shape with the deepest water, at about 6 metres, being in the centre. The tarn looks dark and peated from above, yet when fully immersed in it and peering up through the water it is crystal clear. The tarn is 'blind' as it has no visible in or outflow and is fed by run-off from the back wall and seems to release water from small seeps further down the fell. Blind Tarn is one of a handful of perfect swimming spots that are 'hidden in plain sight' as it is not immediately obvious as to how to get there, and in my experience at least, always offers crowd-free swimming in a wonderful setting.

Many times, I have contemplated a steep traverse across Blind Tarn Screes as a shortcut to Goat's Water ❸ and even attempted it once, to no avail. It was too slow and precarious and even the sheep avoid it, although it would be a fine place for goats. The only sensible way to reach Goat's Water is to backtrack to Torver Bridge and ascend to the tarn via The Cove path. Although much height is lost, and then energetically gained again, one can at least be satisfied that this path offers the best approach views of Dow Crag, dubbed by Wainwright as "second only to Scafell Crag in the magnificence of its rock architecture". To scramble up from The Cove and look upon Goat's Water beneath the crag for the first time is a sight to behold.

Goat's Water sits in an elongated cirque between The Old Man of Coniston and Dow Crag, with Goat's Hause at its head. It is an oligotrophic lake, having very scant nutrient levels and little sediment, both adding to its extraordinary clarity. The water is 12 metres deep in the centre and has steeply sloping sides to the east and west, much less so to the north and south. Great boulders from the crags lie everywhere along the western shoreline, with many lying sentinel in the tarn, like icebergs with only their tips poking out of the water.

The stories of Harry Griffin and the Coniston Tigers have captivated me since childhood. These working-class cragsmen of the 1930s pioneered rock climbing on these very crags, and it is a thrill to look up at Dow Crag from the water and remember my own adventures climbing up there, emulating my heroes. During my last visit, when looking down at the tarn on a very gloomy day, the sun suddenly came out and shot light through the water, illuminating it with a deep Prussian blue so vivid it took my breath away. Places like this seem to amplify the mood of the mountains and accordingly our emotions. No matter how popular they may be with visitors, they remain very special, wild places.

The downhill romp back down to Torver is easy on the legs and allows the walker the luxury of having the time and energy to look about and really appreciate their surroundings. Along the way it is hard not to notice Tranearth Pool glinting seductively at the base of Bannishead Quarry ❺. The disused quarry is lined with birch, rowan and warning signs! A white cascade falls at the head of the quarry, its vertical descent at odds with the diagonal strata of the dark grey slate behind, the stain of orange iron ore weeping from its seams. Although obviously a post-industrial quarry, the place is beautiful. The pool is very popular with locals during the summer who ignore the warning signs with gay abandon. It is up to the visitor to make their own appraisal of the risks of swimming here and if they decide to take a swim, to take great care on the unstable and precarious descent down to the waters edge. I do not recommend swimming here, but can hardly blame you if you do, it always looks so inviting!

Once back down at Torver the tired swim hiker can perhaps enjoy the friendly hospitality of The Wilsons Arms, the best pub in the area. There are however, many alternative options for refreshment to choose from, all detailed in the Information section at the start of this chapter.

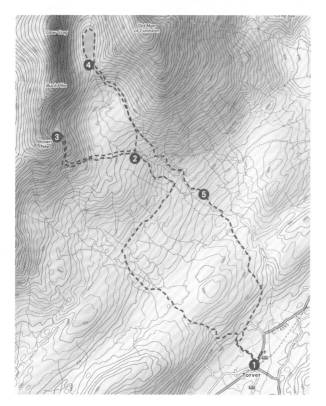

the stepping stones over the beck to follow the path in a northerly direction for about 60 metres, past more quarry remains, before following the path north-east which shadows the wall bordering the Frank Tranearth and Eddy Scale land. The path continues on for over a kilometre from the beck crossing and is covered with bog and fern. Follow the wall all of the way.

At the small track leading north, just before Torver Beck is reached, head straight up the fellside. This track trends north-west up the side of a re-entrant and soon leads to Torver Bridge on the Walna Scar Road.
**2.5 miles**

❷ From the Bridge, head west on the broad bridleway of the Walna Scar Road as it climbs to the pike above. Just before reaching the steep section leading up the side of Brown Pike, look out for a broad re-entrant heading north, north-east on the right where the gill has eroded a deep 'V' up to the side of the track. Look also for the ruined slate building and workings directly above. The path is not obvious at first but once you have found the beginning it provides a nice route straight up to Blind Tarn (ignore the small pathways leading steeply up to the old mine buildings; unless you want to climb up to look down upon the tarn before visiting it).

Blind Tarn has good access to the water all the way around its circumference.
**0.8 miles**

❶ From Torver Village Hall walk along the road past the Church House and cross the road to The Wilsons Arms taking the footpath that runs alongside it and passes their campsite. Stone walls funnel the path up towards the fell. Go straight ahead at the footpath crossroads, through the gate and passing a white cottage where the path cuts back on itself heading west through pine woodland. Follow the path through the woods and up and onto boggy land, keeping on the obvious

walled path that continues on past the wall boundary of Wide Close and onto boggy ground, always heading north-west, and over the warped wooden bridge.

The indistinct footpath threads through sphagnum and rush following Ash Gill Beck which cascades nearby. Continue to the left side of a tree-lined ravine. Ignore the inviting double stiles at the head of Matthew Tranearth meadow. Pass the old quarry workings and spoil heaps before dropping down to take

**3** From Blind Tarn retrace your steps to Torver Bridge. From the bridge, head roughly north over the fell following the light trod of a path which cuts a corner off and saves a bit of time. After 200 metres or so the main path to Goat's Water is reached. Stay on this good path along relatively level ground until it begins to ascend to the scramble between the rocks beneath Goat Crag. Stay on the path which leads directly to Goat's Water.

Goat's Water can be accessed most of the way around but the jumble of rocks around its edge are hard on the feet wherever you get in. The best entry point is probably from the south-west shore, accessed by rock hopping over the outflow beck.
**1.5 miles**

**4** From Goat's Water head back to the Walna Scar Road, passing straight over it to continue down the path following Torver Beck. Keep descending and stay left of the craggy ravine ahead. Cross the gill at the stepping stones and keep going until the Tranearth Quarry and its pool are reached (about 750 metres from Walna Scar Road).

The *only* access to the pool, *if you choose to do so*, is via the steep and crumbling north-east corner nearest to the path.
**1.4 miles**

**5** From Tranearth Pool, regain the path that shadows Torver Beck and follow it south-east to the footbridge over the beck and carry on, passing the Lancashire Caving and Climbing Club hut. Stick to the broad bridleway track all the way to Scar Head and take the footpath to the south-west, ignoring the road in the opposite direction. This will bring you to the path that skirts The Wilsons Arms campground, past the pub and back to Torver village.
**1.5 miles**

**Text & photos:**
Pete Kelly
**Editor:**
Rae Malenoir
**Cover illustration:**
James Lewis
**Design and layout:**
Amy Bolt
**Proofreading:**
Sophie Carran
**Mapping powered by:**

cycle.travel

**Published by:**
Wild Things Publishing Ltd
Bath, BA2 7WG,
United Kingdom
wildthingspublishing.com

**Acknowledgements:** Our outdoor lives must begin somewhere, and I have my parents Anne and Paul to thank for instilling in me a deep love of outdoor places, and for taking me as a child to many of the lakes and fells featured in this book. So, thanks Mam and Dad, for this and everything else you have given me. There are so many friends and clients who have shared swims, secret spots, tea and cake with us over the years and who have loyally supported our swimming business since we were but fledglings. Thanks to you all, and in particular to Steve Ashworth for being there right at the beginning and to his lovely wife Letty for being our Angle Tarn swim model and regularly supplying the best post-swim bacon sandwiches and coffee in Ambleside. Also, thanks must go to Lou Barber for her friendship and encouragement, who also, along with my brother, Simon Kelly, allowed us to practice our guiding skills on you both down the river all those years ago. Thanks also, to all of the Troutbeck Bridge Masters Monday night swimmers for their excellent company on and off the water and while exploring new swimming locations including coaches Sue Aitken and Claire Wilson, Geordie Mark, Charl Webb, Anne Smith, Tanya Bascombe, Keith 'The Smidge' Midgley, Tony Walker, Kate Goldberg, not forgetting fellow Mermen of Windermere Mike Durkin and Mike 'Calypso' Hicks both of whom are the genuine article and quietly hardcore. Thanks also to Thomas Noblett for his friendship and encouragement and his gracious hospitality following many seriously cold swimming sessions. A special mention must go to Debs Lund for help with the photos taken in the Emerald Pool as well as the generous help of Dangerous Dan King who provided some great photos for this book as well as some unforgettable swimming moments. I must also mention all of the original swim guides that me and Andrea have had the privilege of working and swimming with at Swim the Lakes. They continue to influence and shape our approach to swimming and have always been the best of friends as well as reliable and professional colleagues. Thanks to Lianne Brooks Sanders and her family for their early love and support and to Tors Hamilton, Jacqui Young, Susan and Richard Simpson, Kath Finn, Mel Vause, Mike Budd, Alison Faulconbridge and to the legends who are Head Guide Sarah Knight and Chief Guide, Steve Tonkin. During any publication project, there are always many unseen folk working away in the background without whom nothing would get done. Therry and Ralph Cooper along with Nim Crawford have been the best shop crew a man could ask for, allowing me time to go off galivanting around the Lakes researching routes while they held the fort – thank you. I have also been astonished at the patience and good grace of my publisher Daniel Start and editor Rae Malenoir, thanks for making it happen. Finally, to my fantastic wife Andrea and son William. Only you know what you have had to put up with and I can't thank you enough for the love and support you gave when it really mattered. This book is for you both, I hope it makes you smile.

**Photo credits:** All photos Andrea and Pete Kelly at Swim the Lakes except, with huge thanks: Steve Ashworth at Steve Ashworth Media for photos of Helvellyn, Red Tarn and Eskdale. Lou Barber for photos of Bowscale Tarn, Hodge Close Quarry, the River Esk at Dalegarth Bridge and Stanley Force. Dan King for photos of Scafell, Eskdale and the Duddon Valley. Alan O'Dowd for photos of Bowscale Tarn. Daniel Start for photos of Swindale and Kailpot. Also the following produced under CCBYSA licence: p68, 72 Colin Gregory, p70 Karl and Ali, p98 Robert J Heath, p100 ALHI.

**Other books from Wild Things Publishing**

| | | |
|---|---|---|
| Wild Guide Wales | Wild Swimming Britain | Lost Lanes South |
| Wild Guide Scotland | Wild Swimming France | Lost Lanes Wales |
| Wild Guide Central | Wild Swimming Italy | Lost Lanes West |
| Wild Guide Lakes & Dales | Wild Swimming Spain | Lost Lanes North |
| Wild Guide South-West | Wild Swimming Walks Cornwall | Bikepacking |
| Wild Guide South-East | Wild Swimming Walks Dorset | Magical Britain |
| Wild Guide Scandinavia | Wild Swimming Walks Dartmoor | Wild Running |
| Wild Guide Portugal | Wild Swimming Walks London | Wild Ruins & Wild Ruins B.C. |
| Wild Guide French Alps | Hidden Beaches Britain | Wild Garden Weekends |
| Outdoor Swimming London | Hidden Beaches Spain | Scottish Bothy Bible & Walks |